NECESSARY ANGELS

Paul Klee, *Angelus Novus.*

NECESSARY ANGELS

Tradition and Modernity in Kafka,
Benjamin, and Scholem

ROBERT ALTER

Harvard University Press
Cambridge, Massachusetts

in Association with
Hebrew Union College Press, Cincinnati

1991

The Gustave A. and Mamie W. Efroymson
Memorial Lectures

Delivered at the Hebrew Union College–
Jewish Institute of Religion
in Cincinnati, Ohio, during March 1990

For Leo Lowenthal

a ninetieth birthday gift

CONTENTS

Preface
xi

ONE
Corresponding about Kafka
1

TWO
On Not Knowing Hebrew
25

THREE
The Power of the Text
65

FOUR
Revelation and Memory
93

Notes
123

Index
129

PREFACE

Writing this book proved to be an absorbing process of witnessing the self-discovery of a subject. The argument did not end up where I thought it would, and the materials taught me new things about themselves at every step of the way.

Kafka, Benjamin, and Scholem had all figured in my own recurrent concerns as a critic since the 1960s. I am grateful for having enjoyed a cordial relationship with Gershom Scholem, the only one of the three writers it would have been chronologically possible for me to know personally. He gave me generous encouragement in 1969 when I made a first tentative attempt to write about Benjamin. (The essays I wrote around that time on Benjamin and Scholem are reprinted in my book *Defenses of the Imagination*.) In the 1969 essay on Benjamin, I duly noted the profound spiritual affinity between Benjamin and Kafka and also alluded to a certain connection between both and the Hebrew writer S. Y. Agnon. The first chapter here tries to provide some definition for the Kafka-Agnon nexus as it was perceived by both Benjamin and Scholem. What I could not have known twenty years ago, because the Benjamin-Scholem correspondence was still unpublished and several of Scholem's important addresses were as yet undelivered, was how absolutely central Kafka was to Scholem's inner world.

When Professor Michael J. Cook on behalf of the Hebrew Union College, Cincinnati, invited me to give the Gustave A. and Mamie W Efroymson Lectures for 1990, I thought I would carry out a "triangulation" of Kafka, Benjamin, and Scholem, but at the time I proposed the topic, it wasn't altogether clear to me what I would actually do with it. There was an intriguing anomaly, or perhaps only a coincidence, involved. Kafka is rightly thought of as the exemplary modernist among writers of prose fiction. Benjamin has come increasingly to be regarded as one of the century's major literary critics and speculative observers of the quandaries of modernity. Scholem's stature as one of the leading historians of the age is firmly established. Benjamin and Scholem were intimate friends, and both were continually fascinated by Kafka. All three writers grew up in highly assimilated German-speaking homes, and all three rebelled against the cultural values of their fathers by seeking, in rather divergent ways, to realize a serious encounter with the Jewish tradition left behind by the fathers.

One of my initial ideas was to try to show how these three German-Jewish intellectuals, precisely because they situated themselves in a liminal realm between tradition and modernity, were able to work out in their respective literary vehicles a probing vision of the dilemmas of modernity. In this regard, all were, as I have said of Kafka, exemplary figures, though by no means typical ones. Something of this original intention to render an account of the Jewish writer as exemplary modernist is detectable in the chapters that follow. I also originally imagined, perhaps influenced by the theological auspices of the Efroymson Lectures, that I would consider the relevance to the three writers of sweeping theological categories such as revelation, divine language, law, and exegesis. The reader will readily discern here the vestiges of that metaphysical scheme. What I discovered, however, as I shuttled back and forth among the texts of the three writers was that the specific biographical data and the concrete historical setting of their sundry literary enterprises were more deeply interesting, more revelatory, than all such conceptual generalities, or rather, that the general categories could be understood coherently only by seeing their intricate roots in the lives of the writers. It also became apparent that grand pronouncements about moder-

nity had to give way to observations about the distinctive
cultural moment of German-speaking Jewry in the early decades of this century.

What began to unfold, then, as I reread Kafka, Benjamin,
and Scholem was a kind of phenomenological description of
the characteristic "structures of consciousness" of these intense
post-traditional Jews emerging from the modern German setting. The argument gradually shifted its illustrative grounds
from the major works of fiction, critical synthesis, and historiography—although of course these could in no way be ignored—to the letters, the diaries and notebooks, the gnomic
and fragmentary pieces of all three writers. In the light shed by
these materials, the sheer serendipity of the subject became
progressively clear. It emerged that there were not merely
loose correspondences between writer and writer but an elaborate network of images, concepts, and imaginative processes
that drew them together. These shared elements, which con-
stituted a kind of watermark of the imagination for all three,
were not limited to broad intellectual concerns, such as their
common affinity for the Kabbalah, but also were instructively
manifested in seemingly adventitious details—an odd focus
on alphabets and the physical act of inscription, a fascination
with the very idea of texts and the notion that textuality was
the vehicle of truth, a beguilement by images of angels. All
this led me to see something unanticipated—that the interar-
ticulation of Kafka, Benjamin, and Scholem brought out a
dimension of the work of each not apparent in scrutinizing
each of them separately. Readers, of course, will have to judge
for themselves whether that is persuasively the case, but what I
try to do here is to show how the rigorously unsentimental
nostalgia of all three writers for the conceptual and spiritual
world of Jewish tradition gave at once a distinctive direction
to their writing and a special acuteness to their apprehension
of modernity.

Let me add that this claim does not involve the slightest

pretension of having found the magic key to any of these writers. The engagement with Judaism was obviously decisive for Scholem, devoted Zionist and master historian of Jewish mysticism, and there is considerable biographical evidence that it was almost equally so for Kafka, although explicitly Jewish themes almost never appear on the surface of his fiction. It was also a lifelong concern of Benjamin's, but with a good deal of intermittence, as he concentrated on the realm of modern European cultural experience and as his early Jewish messianism was translated into a Marxist scheme of historical redemption. In any case, my own focus here on the background of Jewish tradition should not be construed as a demotion of the importance of other backgrounds: Flaubert, Kierkegaard, German Expressionism for Kafka; neo-Kantianism and Marxism for Benjamin; German philology and (despite his own denial of the connection) Nietzsche for Scholem. Contexts, as contemporary literary theorists remind us, are infinitely extendable, and with all the mountains of secondary literature on Kafka and the rapidly growing bibliographies on Benjamin and, to a lesser extent, on Scholem, there is no doubt more to say about the multiple intellectual backgrounds of each. Many pertinent perspectives, then, are not even intimated in my exposition, which attempts solely to define the Jewish matrix of the three writers. If that definition is in some degree successful, it may tell us something about the enterprise of the three writers, about their perception of the modern condition, and perhaps even about the dilemmas of Judaism after the breakdown of the traditional world of faith.

I want to thank the faculty of the Hebrew Union College for providing the stimulus for this study by inviting me to deliver the Efroymson Lectures, and for all the kindnesses shown me during my stay in Cincinnati in March 1990. (The three lectures given there basically correspond to Chapters Two and Three of the book.) Chapter One appeared in a slightly different form in *The New Republic,* and I am grateful to its editors for granting me the rights to that material. Work on the project was made possible by a sabbatical salary supplement paid from the funds of the Class of 1937 Chair in Comparative Literature at the University of California at Berkeley, and secretarial costs were also provided from the same source. The typescript was prepared with admirable patience and attention to detail by Janet Livingstone. I am especially grateful to Michael Bernstein for reading the draft version and encouraging me, with all the force of his informed grasp of the subject, about the value of the undertaking.

The lines from "Angel Surrounded by Paysans," copyright 1950 by Wallace Stevens, are reprinted from *The Collected Poems of Wallace Stevens* by permission of Alfred A. Knopf, Inc. The quotations from "A Dream" in the text, from *Franz Kafka: The Complete Stories,* edited by Nahum N. Glatzer, are reprinted by permission of Schocken Books, published by Pantheon Books, a Division of Random House, Inc., copyright 1946, 1947, 1948, 1949, 1954, © 1958, 1971 by Schocken Books, Inc. The frontispiece, Paul Klee's *Angelus Novus* (pen, ink, and pastel; 1920), is reproduced by courtesy of the Israel Museum, Jerusalem.

Berkeley
April 1990

Yet I am the necessary angel of earth,
Since, in my sight, you see the earth again,

Cleared of its stiff and stubborn, man-locked set,
And in my hearing, you hear its tragic drone

Rise liquidly in liquid lingerings,
Like watery words awash; like meanings said

By repetitions of half-meanings.

Wallace Stevens,
"Angel Surrounded by Paysans"

ONE

CORRESPONDING ABOUT KAFKA

ʃʃ

I'm convinced by what you write about Kafka. During the weeks I've spent considering the problem as closely as possible, ideas have occurred to me that correspond strictly to yours.

> Walter Benjamin to Gershom Scholem,
> October 3, 1931

The relationship between Walter Benjamin and Gershom Scholem is surely one of the extraordinary intellectual friendships of the twentieth century. It is not only that each was an innovative thinker of the first order—Benjamin as critic, Scholem as historian—transforming the intellectual horizons of his field, or that they wrestled for twenty-five years over intellectual and spiritual issues which still seem compellingly urgent; it is also that, on a human level, the moral fiber of their friendship proved so tough and resilient despite their drastically divergent personal paths and despite the most soul-trying historical circumstances. To the end, they continued to share the intellectual passions of their student years; they never hesitated to challenge one another, even when the difference between them was painful, as when Benjamin dismayed Scholem by moving, however ambiguously, from a metaphysical to a Marxist perspective. They never ceased to make the highest demands of each other because they always had the highest expectations of each other's gifts. Whatever their divergences of viewpoint and loyalty, each steadily felt toward the other a love for the person and a generously affectionate admiration for his mind. It may be that in the last dozen years of their relationship Scholem tended at times to assume the high ground of authority and Benjamin allowed him to play the role of his own Jewish superego. Nevertheless, the profound mutual respect they felt was never undermined, and Scholem's subsequent devotion to Benjamin's posthumous legacy was unflagging.

Scholem and Benjamin first met in their native Berlin in

the summer of 1915, when Scholem was seventeen and a half
and Benjamin twenty-three. At the time, both were deeply
involved in the ideological debates of the German student
movement of those years; both were in a process of vehement
rebellion against the complacencies of their own assimilated
German-Jewish bourgeois background, each having determined to confront the world with what Scholem in his memoir
of their friendship would call "radical demands"—demands
that each in his own way continued to make throughout his
life. In Scholem's case, this rebellion had already manifested
itself as an uncompromising rejection of assimilation—the
adoption of Zionism, an immersion in Hebrew (which he had
managed to master in a scant two years), the study of the
Talmud and other Jewish sources. Benjamin, chiefly through
Scholem, repeatedly contemplated undertaking all three of
these courses, at least for the next fifteen years, but the sphere
of activity that continued to allure him was that of German
and French culture. Yet even in the most ardent moments of
his never quite consummated affair with Communism, his
fascination with Judaism did not flag—an involvement that
made him vaguely suspect in the eyes of the Marxists, including his problematic friend, Bertolt Brecht.

In the years after their first encounter, Benjamin and Scholem spent an increasing amount of time together, including an
extended period in 1918 and 1919 in Switzerland, where
Benjamin was living with his wife, Dora, in daily domestic
storms into which Scholem was inadvertently drawn. After
their return to Germany they were together intermittently,
and the volume of their correspondence begins to swell. The
intimacy marked in the letters grows by slow stages: at first,
Scholem is addressed as "Herr Scholem," then as "Dear Gerhard," but still with the formal *Sie*, and only beginning in
mid-1921 with the intimate *Du*. After Scholem's emigration to
Palestine in 1924, their relationship was entirely epistolary
with the exception of two brief reunions in Paris, the first in

1927 and the second in 1938, just two years before Benjamin ended his own life when he thought he was being turned back at the Spanish border in his attempt to flee Nazi-occupied France.

A two-volume edition of Benjamin's correspondence was published in Germany in 1966 (it is as yet unavailable in English), edited by Scholem and Theodor Adorno.[1] From 1917 onward, the overwhelming majority of the letters are addressed to Scholem—although, since Benjamin had other correspondents who were not so meticulous in preserving everything he sent them, the published correspondence does not entirely represent the variety of his epistolary connections. Because Scholem retained copies of only five of the handwritten letters he sent to Benjamin, his half of the correspondence does not appear. Benjamin was equally a paper-saver (just as both men were passionate bibliophiles), but when he fled Berlin in March 1933, the Nazi authorities seized all his papers and none survived. His final flight, this time from Paris, in 1940, left behind another set of papers, duly confiscated by the Gestapo, which were preserved because they were accidentally stuck into the file of the *Pariser Tageszeitung*. At the end of the war they were transferred to Russia and, later, to the archives of the German Democratic Republic in Potsdam. Scholem learned about the existence of these papers and in 1966, was allowed to examine them in the GDR archives, where he discovered all of his own letters to Benjamin from 1933 onward. He was promised photocopies, but Communist bureaucratic caprice intervened, and it was only eleven years later, around the time of his eightieth birthday, that the copies were unexpectedly delivered. Through this moment of relenting on the part of a faceless bureaucracy we possess a precious set of documents of modern intellectual history. The German edition, edited by Scholem, appeared in 1980, two years before his death; the letters are now also available in a generally competent English version.[2] It is a book that combines brilliant philosophic and cultural speculation and argumentation with the poignancy of autobiography, holding up a luminous mirror to dark times.

Even in the one-sided form in which it has been preserved, the early phase of the correspondence, before Scholem's emigration, often has the quality of an untiring afterclass continuation of a seminar discussion by two ferociously bright graduate students. Benjamin, obviously responding to a series of proposals in what must have been equally voluminous letters from Scholem, pursues definitions and distinctions in an effort to understand Kant's theory of knowledge, cubism and the status of representation in painting, Franz Rosenzweig's theology, the nature of language, and much else. There is a certain brash confidence in Benjamin's early letters that was no doubt shared by Scholem: the two were clearly impatient with the superficiality of most of their teachers and contemporaries, acting almost as though they were the only two good minds in the neighborhood (a youthful extravagance with a good degree of justification).

The two-way correspondence, spanning the years 1933–1940, shows both men in a more sober and indeed sometimes somber caste of spirit. This shift was equally a consequence of what was happening in the world and of the stage of life at which they had arrived. The Germany that had intellectually nurtured them had been taken over by the forces of barbarism. Benjamin was in exile in France, eking out a living from freelance journalism and a modest stipend from the eclectic-Marxist Institute for Social Research, which had migrated from Frankfurt to New York—sometimes so reduced in circumstances that he could barely afford stationery on which to write his letters. Because of his poverty and his persistent marginality, he had contemplated the possibility of suicide as early as 1931; with Hitler's advent, he repeatedly brooded over the prospect of a new world war in which, perhaps through the agency of poison gas, humanity would be annihilated.

Scholem, whose beeline "from Berlin to Jerusalem" (the title of his partial autobiography) stood in contrast to Benjamin's vocational zigzags, was secure enough professionally and economically in his professorship of Jewish mysticism at the Hebrew University, founded the year after his arrival in Palestine. But the Zionist community there was profoundly shaken by the sustained waves of murderous Arab attacks against it that began in 1936. Although Scholem wanted to cling to the idea of a binational Jewish-Arab state, it became increasingly clear to him that there would be no peaceful solution to the conflict of the two communities in Palestine, and all that he had hoped for from Zionism in regard to Jewish spiritual renewal seemed to be frustrated by the internal divisions, the shortsightedness, the extremism, and the strident politicking within the Zionist movement, at the very moment when European Jewry was being isolated and ominously threatened. If Benjamin was an ardent devotee of European culture utterly despairing of its future, Scholem, at least at some points, was no less despairing of the future of Zionism. Thus, just sixty days before the outbreak of World War II, he writes Benjamin from Jerusalem that the experience of the last six years leaves no grounds for hope that revolution will solve mankind's problems. "The workers' movement as a revolutionary political factor is deader than a dead dog, there is no point in upholding any illusions on this point." So much for Benjamin's political pieties (which, according to those close to him at the time, he had finally renounced with a sense of relief after the Molotov-Ribbentrop Pact). As for Scholem's own pieties:

> . . . the future of Judaism is totally cloaked in darkness: it cannot pretend to be invisible—inactive and asleep—as others may (perhaps) try to do, because it will no longer have the bodily basis of an existence which is still at the disposal of the vanquished socialists. We aren't able to make alliances any longer, since there is no one left who might be interested in doing so. We must not give up on this generation, and since nothing could replace

Palestine in its function for Judaism but empty phrases evocative
of nothing, how should I conceive of the years to come? In this
darkness I only know how to be silent.[3]

The letters of Benjamin and Scholem are written out of a
certain sense of loneliness stoically sustained—not quite isolation but the loneliness of genius pursuing its solitary way
against the grain of the times, making "radical demands" that
political reality would not meet. In 1930–31, after Benjamin
finally renounced his long-deferred scheme of learning Hebrew and coming to Palestine, Scholem wrote his friend three
remarkable letters, of which he made copies, and which appear in the two-volume *Briefe*. (It is a pity that' this whole
exchange was not added to the English edition of the two-way
correspondence.) In the last of these, dated May 6, 1931,
Scholem shrewdly observes, "You are endangered more by
your desire for community, even if it be the apocalyptic community of the revolution, than by the horror of loneliness that
speaks from so many of your writings." Scholem on his part
had sought to discover community in his personal return to
Zion. Professionally, the endeavor was clearly successful, and
by the late 1930s he could say to Benjamin with pride, and
with ample justification, that a "school of Scholem" had gathered round him in Jerusalem. Politically and spiritually, he
remained, despite a few like-minded friends, almost as much
of a queer duck among the Zionists as Benjamin in the 1930s
was among the Marxists. And it is far from clear whether he
ever became as close to anyone in Jerusalem as he had been to
Benjamin in Germany.

What both men had as compensation—if one can speak in
such cases of compensation—was a burning sense of intellectual vocation, offering them, as it were, the embrace of pos-
terity in lieu of the community of their contemporaries. Benjamin turned forty in 1932; Scholem reached that age in 1937;
and their letters in these years are marked by the feeling that

the time had come in both their lives to produce the master-works of which they knew themselves capable. Since the early 1920s, Scholem had been doing the spadework for the modern scholarly investigation of Jewish mysticism through a series of close textual studies and specialized monographs. Now, he informed Benjamin on June 28, 1935, he was prepared to undertake a "fairly voluminous . . . stocktaking" of these fifteen years of labor. "There'll be no lack of amazing and very amazing things," he wrote jauntily, "and the historical observer is guaranteed to get his money's worth." Six years later, through the unexpected mediation of the series of lectures he had been invited to present in New York in 1938, the stocktaking would appear as *Major Trends in Jewish Mysticism,* one of the magisterial modern works of the historical imagination. It was dedicated to the memory of Walter Benjamin.

In his reply (August 9, 1935) to the letter that announced the project of the future *Major Trends,* Benjamin offered Scholem a tantalizing prospectus of the book that he called first *Passagen* (Parisian Arcades) and then *Paris, Capital of the Nineteenth Century:* "The work represents both the philosophical application of surrealism—and thereby its sublation [*Aufhebung*]—as well as the attempt to retain the image of history in the most inconspicuous corners of existence—the detritus of history, as it were." What Benjamin meant by this gnomic formulation may perhaps be inferred from the fragments of *Passagen* that he actually wrote, and from his two late essays on Baudelaire.

In his critical exposition of Baudelaire, the argument often proceeds through a movement of free association, like Surrealist poetry. Thus, the frenetic Parisian crowd in Baudelaire's poems carries Benjamin to the carnival mob in the paintings of James Ensor, to the brutal alliance of police and looters in totalitarian states, to the invention of the match, of snapshot photography, and of the cinema, whereby "the human sensorium [is] subjected to a complex training . . . of perception in the form of shocks." As we are swept from Baudelaire's poetry to the broad forces and the odd minutiae of modern history, Surrealist free association is "sublated"—negated, heightened, and sustained—because it is made the vehicle of what aspires to be a rigorous historical-philosophical analysis.[4]

The project was powerfully original, but given the harried conditions of Benjamin's existence and the anguished oscillations of his inner life, it is not surprising that it was never realized. Only his essays on Baudelaire and a large stack of fascinating notes and fragments, published long after his death, in 1982, suggest what the work might have been. The aphoristic, sometimes telegraphic fragments deploy Marxist notions of market, production, commodity, and consumer, though turned on the idiosyncratic wheel of Benjamin's gnomic speculations that could sometimes transmute conceptual straw into gold. The Baudelaire essays, with their riveting account of the "decay of experience" in the modern urban realm that is reflected in Baudelaire's new poetics of shock, seem closer to the program of a philosophical application of Surrealism, using a kind of lyric impressionism punctuated with bold aphorisms, in order to illuminate the unconscious of a cultural era.

The Arcades project preoccupied Benjamin for the last thirteen years of his life. Some scholars have inferred that the battered briefcase he was desperately clutching, according to one witness, when he sought to cross the Spanish border the day before he took his own life, contained a partial manuscript of this long-projected work. (The briefcase mysteriously disappeared.) The surviving fragments of the Arcades project, however, look suspiciously like the Sisyphean notes and documentation for an impossible undertaking: to apply the Surrealist technique of montage to nineteenth-century Paris in a way that would yield a philosophical analysis of historical process, exposing the meretricious myths of bourgeois society and highlighting the utopian potential of collective imagination.[5] Both Benjamin and Scholem were fascinated with fragments. Scholem devoted his life to expounding a body of lore that was intrinsically fragmentary, or at the very least antisystematic. The power of his work is his success in conceptually defining a system from this welter of literary scraps, though some of his critics have accused him of imposing system where it may not exist. Benjamin's aim was the converse: to preserve the fragmentariness of his materials through the mobility of montage, combining constant quotation with aphoristic observation, and thus allowing systematic thought to emerge from juxtaposition itself. Perhaps the task was in the end undoable.

Understandably enough, Benjamin, unlike Scholem, was sometimes troubled by doubts about whether he would ever have an audience and whether there was any point to writing. "What will we leave behind someday," he observed gloomily toward the end (February 4, 1939), "other than our own writings with their uncut pages?" But at the beginning of his last letter to Scholem, from occupied France, on January 11, 1940, he urged his friend to publish his New York lectures as soon as possible: "Every line we succeed in publishing today—no matter how uncertain the future to which we entrust it—is a victory wrenched from the powers of darkness." The exhortation was no empty rhetorical gesture. Writing like theirs was an unflinching effort to grasp the complex dialectical nature—a favored term of Scholem's, *sans* materialism—of historical reality, to define the wonderful architectonic structures that man's imagination erects over against, or upon, the abyss of mortality and the dissolution of value that underlies human existence (see, for example, Benjamin's account of German Baroque tragic drama, Scholem's explorations of Sabbatianism and Lurianic Kabbalah). At a moment when the murderous simplification of totalitarian ideology had displaced historical realities with schematic lies used as the warrant for a program of annihilation, the intellectual enterprises of Scholem and Benjamin were an act of cultural resistance, the delicate sustaining of a rich legacy that totalitarianism hoped to wipe out forever.

There was one modern writer, arguably the greatest of the twentieth-century architects of the abyss, who spoke profoundly to the spiritual condition shared by Benjamin and Scholem. Franz Kafka, a decade older than either of them, was in effect the lonely pioneer of their whole generation of modernist intellectuals, at least in the German-speaking sphere, though he surely aspired to found no school. He also marked the crucial point of intersection of the interests of the two friends. As a rigorously iconoclastic modernist in the medium of fiction, he powerfully embodied the new poetics of disjuncture, discontinuity, and purposeful perplexity that fascinated Benjamin. As a writer hyperconscious of the categories of a no longer authoritative Jewish tradition, he exposed both the power and the atrophy of tradition and theological authority that equally preoccupied Scholem and Benjamin. Scholem, moreover, was strongly inclined to see Kafka as a latter-day kabbalist exhibiting deep kinship with some of the esoteric figures he had studied as a historian—a notion he broached to Benjamin and spelled out much later in his "Ten Unhistorical Theses on the Kabbalah." (Harold Bloom, impishly and suggestively, though also somewhat misleadingly, has proposed that Scholem's reading of the Kabbalah was to a large extent *determined* by the strong early influence of Kafka.)[6] Benjamin and Scholem express their avid admiration of Kafka in their correspondence as early as the later 1920s, when it was difficult to locate any of his works in the bookstores. In the two-way correspondence from 1933 onward, they constantly return to the subject of Kafka. The illuminating comments on both sides culminate in the extraordinary essay-length letter on Kafka that Benjamin sent to Scholem in New York on June 12, 1938. One of his most arresting contributions to the criticism of modern literature, he hoped Scholem would show it to the publisher Salman Schocken and perhaps help him obtain a remunerative contract for a book; but it also remains an intimate communication to a friend about a topic that mattered deeply to both of them.

The discussions of Kafka in the correspondence are accompanied by the shadow presence, occasionally evoked explicitly, of a kind of literary twin whose contours may not be very clear to the ordinary Western reader. Scholem had become friendly with S. Y. Agnon, who would prove to be the one major Hebrew modernist writer, in the course of Agnon's extended sojourn in Germany during and after World War I. They both made the move to Jerusalem around the same time and remained lifelong friends. Benjamin met Agnon through Scholem in 1920 and became a keen admirer. Reading Agnon's stories in German translations (a few of them done by Scholem), he was convinced that Agnon was one of the masters of contemporary fiction, and looked forward eagerly to every scrap of his work that became available in German. Benjamin and Scholem shared the perception that there was a deep imaginative kinship between Agnon and Kafka. Scholem, in a brief observation in the *Jüdische Rundschau* in 1928, had broached the idea that Agnon's fiction worked out a revision of Kafka's *Trial*: both drew an apocalyptic sense of reality from their powerful realization of a child's vision, but Agnon's fiction managed to hold out a possibility of redemption.[7]

In conversation, at least half-seriously, the two friends had raised the possibility of Benjamin's writing a comparative essay on Agnon and Kafka. On January 18, 1934, Benjamin appears to propose (at any rate, according to Scholem's construal of this sentence) that Scholem undertake this task instead of him: "Agnon displays mastery in every piece, and if I had become 'a teacher in Israel'—but I could have just as easily become an ant lion—I would not have been able to refrain from a lecture on Agnon and Kafka."

In Hebrew criticism after the 1950s, comparisons between Agnon and Kafka would become commonplace, but at least on

the surface the early Agnon and Kafka look like polar op-
posites. Agnon was the product of a highly literate Orthodox
home in a middle-sized Galician town. The keen interest he
later developed in German and European culture, which he
generally camouflaged in his fiction, was always that of the
autodidact outsider. He wrote in a flagrantly archaizing Hebrew steeped in the associations and values of three millennia
of tradition, worlds away from the limpid German muting the
historical resonances of the language that Kafka fashioned for
his fiction. Most crucially, the bulk of Agnon's fiction in his
first quarter-century as a writer—his earliest stories were published around 1905—seemed to be ventriloquistic performances of the voices of Jewish tradition—tales of Torah
scribes, yeshiva students, unworldly pious talmudists, crafts-
men of synagogue art, suffused with the intricate lore of a
vanishing world of faith. These artful redeployments of traditional storytelling show no obvious family resemblance to
"The Judgment," *The Trial*, "The Metamorphosis," "In the Penal
Colony." Agnon had also written some stories and novellas of
a Flaubertian caste, enacted in modern settings, and in 1935 he
would publish his psychological masterpiece, *A Simple Story*,
but these were not available to Benjamin in translation. At the
very moment when Benjamin was writing Scholem about the
irresistible temptation to produce an essay on Agnon and
Kafka, the Hebrew writer had in fact begun to publish a series
of disjunct, dreamlike, "Kafkaesque" stories (he always vehemently denied any influence) that he would later put together
as *The Book of Deeds*, but Benjamin probably did not even know
of their existence. Some understanding of the subterranean
connections Benjamin and Scholem intuited between the two
writers may throw light on the evolving perception they
shared through the years of Kafka as the posttraditional Jewish writer who above all others mapped out the spiritual
territory of the modern condition.

In the letter of January 18, 1934, which I have already mentioned, Benjamin is gratefully responding to a small volume of Agnon's stories in German translation that Scholem had sent him. He singles out one piece in particular: "I have yet to find anything more beautiful in his works than 'The Great Synagogue,' which I regard as a tremendous masterpiece." At first glance, it is puzzling that this two-and-a-half-page tale—never translated into English—of the discovery of a buried synagogue by playing schoolchildren should have made such a profound impression on the critic who celebrated the modernist tensions of Kafka, Proust, Brecht, and the Surrealists.[8] Let me comment briefly on the story, for the complications in its seemingly naive recuperation of the harmonies of pious tradition may tell us something about the Kafka whom Benjamin defined as a creator of Aggadah (lore) without a Halakhah (law), and whom Scholem characterized as the proponent of a latter-day, heretical Kabbalah.

The bare plot outline of "The Great Synagogue" suggests a simple, perhaps nostalgic parable of the recovery of the spiritual glories of the past—a shimmering dream, it should be noted, that, in all its impossibility, never ceased to have an allure for Benjamin, even at the height of his Marxist phase. The children, digging on a mountainside where they are, pointedly, playing a messianic game of pretending to rebuild the ancient Temple, discover shingles buried in the soil. It soon becomes clear that there is a whole roof just below the surface of the ground. A major excavation is initiated by the community; when it is completed, the Great Synagogue of the town of Jaslowitz stands revealed in all its antique splendor—a structure whose very existence had been no more than a bare inference from certain geographic indications in old Hebrew responsa. This resurgence of the pious past is accompanied by a miraculous event. When the whole building is unearthed, the door is found to be locked, and no locksmith's tool can budge it. Then a voice is heard from within chanting, "How goodly are thy tents, O Jacob!" (the first words of the morning service), and the portal swings open.

Benjamin must have admired the understated beauty with which this vision of recuperation is conveyed, but I suspect he was also impressed by other, countervailing lines of force in the story. To begin with, the schoolchildren are clearly not a realistic representation of Galician *heder* kids but a flagrantly fanciful ideal projection: the games they play are straight out of the Bible and the Mishnah; they undertake their rebuilding of the Temple the day after the fast of Tisha B'Av, which commemorates the Temple's destruction, singing, as they dabble in the mud, the Passover hymn that begins, "The Almighty will soon rebuild his house." The Great Synagogue itself is confused in the story with two antithetical structures. When only the roof has been uncovered, people think it may be the castle in which a local lord is said to have shut up all his wife's lovers, leaving them to perish by asphyxiation. Then, as stained-glass windows are revealed, the building is thought to be an old church, and the Jews are temporarily banished from the excavation. Thus, before the full emergence of the house of prayer, its site is marked in public surmise by murder, promiscuity, and an alien cult (the three cardinal crimes in rabbinic law). Finally, the Great Synagogue, freed from its casement of earth, is seen resplendent as in days of yore: "And as the August sun shone on the stained-glass windows, everyone was suffused with their light. Ancient days—ancient sanctuaries."

But the final note of the tale marks Agnon's perspective as a contemporary of Benjamin, and of Kafka. The old ark and Torah scrolls have been perfectly preserved: "And twin carved doves spread their wings, the wings of the dove covered with silver, and a great prayerbook was set on the lectern, a prayerbook written in lovely script on deerskin. Everything was in its place, intact. Only the Eternal Light was on the point of going out." The laconic, artful ambiguity of the last sentence is quintessential Agnon. In another miraculous touch, the Eternal Light has continued burning underground through the years. The term used for "going out" also means setting of the sun, so this final image oddly undercuts the previous image of the synagogue refulgent with sunlight. There is probably a biblical resonance—the "lamp of God" that has "not yet gone out" when young Samuel is called in the night by God in 1 Samuel 3. An optimistic reader might infer that the Great Synagogue has been recovered just in time to replenish the Eternal Light before it gutters. Another inference, perhaps more likely, given the wording, is that the Eternal Light is in fact about to go out: the wondrous renewal of the past presents a soul-stirring spectacle, but it comes too late in the history of faith and culture—the return can no longer take place.

Closely scrutinized, "The Great Synagogue," like most of the ostensibly traditionalist stories of the early Agnon, reveals not a reversal of the process of judgment in Kafka, as Scholem had contended in 1928, but its inexorable working out in the guise of tradition. To put this a little differently, in Agnon the theological enchantment of the world of piety is elaborately and lovingly evoked at the same time that it is ironically subverted from within. Kafka's case is the obverse: his gray fictional landscapes of pathetic animals and petty bureaucrats (the difference between the two is not substantive) have been ruthlessly shorn of all the outward trappings of tradition, but the classic Jewish triad of revelation, law, and commentary virtually defines his imaginative world, whose protagonists at once cannot do without these categories and cannot understand them, tolerate them, live by them. Over the years, despite vehement differences on particular issues of definition, this is a perception about Kafka that Benjamin and Scholem shared, grasping the full range of its implications, I think, better than any other of Kafka's critics.

They disagreed strenuously, for example, about whether revelation was absent from Kafka's world, as Benjamin had intimated in his 1934 essay on Kafka, or whether it was present but impossible to fulfill, as Scholem, recalling the more nihilistic manifestations of the Kabbalah, argued in his letter of July 17, 1934. (In my last chapter, I will try to explain why this particular point of dispute should have seemed so urgent, especially to Scholem.) What is remarkable about these exchanges on Kafka, which continued down to the last year of their correspondence, is that the two men, even in partial difference, are able to carry out a process of collaborative thinking, the perspectives of Benjamin, metaphysician without a tradition, and Scholem, historian of a mystical countertradition, beautifully complementing each other. Benjamin's extraordinary 1938 essay-letter on Kafka, seen against the background of a decade of correspondence on the subject, is a culmination of this collaboration, though Scholem objected to its emphasis on failure in Kafka and argued that some of the features Benjamin claimed to be distinctive of Kafka were intrinsic to mystical tradition as such.

The first extended communication between the two on Kafka is a letter Scholem wrote, in response to an invitation from Benjamin to share his ideas on the author of *The Trial*, on August 1, 1931. (The letter does not appear in the published correspondence, but it was preserved among Benjamin's notes on Kafka, and Scholem reproduces it entire in *Walter Benjamin: The Story of a Friendship*.)[9] Both friends, it should be said, had a marked tendency to think about Kafka in metaphysically weighted aphorisms. In this initial document of their exchange, Scholem worries away at what he calls "the theological secret of perfect prose" in Kafka. Let me suggest that the perfection of prose is an important dimension of the affinity between Kafka and Agnon. As I noted before, they went about the pursuit of stylistic perfection in opposite ways, Agnon fashioning a classical Hebrew redolent of the foundational texts of the early rabbis. Both writers, interestingly, were inspired by the exacting standards of the prose of Flaubert, but the effect that both achieved was very different from that of the French writer. In Flaubert's novels, the painstakingly wrought prose is the supreme expression of a purely aesthetic impulse, the magisterial mark of the artificer on his verbal artifice. In Kafka, and in Agnon, as Scholem recognized in his 1931 letter, the perfect prose is an assertion of the voice of authoritative tradition in a world that offers no purchase for such authority: "Kafka's linguistic world . . . with its affinity to the Last Judgment, probably represents the prosaic in its most canonical form." Two years later, in a poem on Benjamin's autobiographical *One-Way Street*, Scholem reflected:

> In the old days all roads led
> To God and his name, somehow.
> We are not pious. [*Wir sind nicht fromm.*]
> We remain in the Profane,
> And where God once stood now stands: Melancholy.[10]

For both of them, Kafka was the writer who gazed unblinking into the heart of this melancholy but at the same time could not help seeing the ghostly lineaments of the landscape of the old days, as K. peers up at the Castle through fog and swirling snow to see nothing and everything, the lunatic creation of a mad child and the towering realm of truth.

Benjamin on his part picks up the notion of "the prosaic in its most canonical form" and links it with the specific narrative and exegetical literary forms of religious tradition. "It is in the attempt to metamorphize life into Scripture that I perceive the meaning of 'reversal' [*Umkehr*], which so many of Kafka's parables endeavor to bring about" (August 11, 1934). The implications of this insight in regard to the ambiguous weight of tradition in Kafka's work are elaborated four years later in the essay-letter: "Kafka eavesdropped on tradition, and he who listens hard does not see." The image is brilliantly chosen, not only because it conveys so effectively Kafka's relation to tradition but also because in fact many of Kafka's protagonists become eavesdroppers (or peeping toms), straining at cracks and crevices to cull a garbled and imperfect version of things that perhaps are not even being said. In all this, Benjamin goes on to say, the "consistency of truth . . . has been lost." Other modern imaginations have come to the same sad recognition, but their typical response has been to cling to some fragment of what they want to regard as truth, regretfully conceding that it may no longer have the coherence or authority to make it transmissible. Kafka's project was more radical. "Kafka's real genius was that he tried something entirely new: he sacrificed truth for the sake of clinging to transmissibility, to its aggadic element." This key perception opens several main corridors in the haunted house of fiction Kafka built: the sense floating through the stories, parables, and novels of a "rumor about the true things (a sort of theology passed on by whispers)," the pervasiveness of folly oddly conjoined with what sometimes look like angelic presences, the restless operation of exegesis in virtually all aspects of the narratives, and the paradox of Kafka's "radiant serenity" in shaping a fictional world that often seems to invite madness or despair.

However much the great letter of June 12, 1938, was a crystallization of what the two men had been thinking together about Kafka over the previous seven years, it is by no means an end point of the discussion. Scholem, as we have seen, was not entirely happy with all of Benjamin's emphases; at the same time, he encouraged him to develop his most important insight: "If you were to succeed in representing the borderline case of wisdom, which Kafka does indeed represent, as the crisis of the sheer transmissibility of the truth, you would have achieved something absolutely magnificent" (November 6–8, 1938). As we shall have occasion to see, the issue of transmissibility, which is the enabling condition of all tradition, was crucial for each of the three writers.

A few months later, Benjamin is turning over a new idea, no more than intimated in the notion of wisdom decayed into folly of his essay-letter—that humor is the ultimate secret of Kafka's tradition-obsessed modernist fiction. He is inclined to put this as a challenge to his friend, just as Scholem had proposed a challenge to him: "I think the key to Kafka's work is likely to fall into the hands of the person who *is able to extract the comic aspects of Jewish theology.* Has there been such a man? Or would you be man enough to be that man?" (February 4, 1939; the emphasis is Benjamin's).

While this long conversation on Kafka continues, the world is of course going to pieces, as both men are acutely aware, though only occasionally do they talk about it directly in their letters. Behind their discussions loom the Arab uprising, the British Mandate's closing down of Jewish immigration to Palestine, the inauguration of the concentration-camp universe (into which both Scholem's brother and Benjamin's disappeared soon after Hitler came to power), Kristallnacht, and, finally, the beginning of the long-dreaded world war. Against this grim background, the Kafka exchange epitomizes what is most humanly impressive about their correspondence. They are not merely scraping on a private fiddle as Rome, Jerusalem, Paris, and Berlin threaten to burst into flames because so much is at stake for them in trying to make sense of Kafka. In their larger intellectual projects, neither was directly concerned with the nature of totalitarianism, as their mutual friend, Hannah Arendt, later would be, but both saw the new century in which they had come of age as an era in which the old sustaining structures of belief, value, and community had been shattered. Benjamin traced this process back to the twin implosive forces of industrialization and urbanization in the nineteenth century; Scholem, following the internal lines of Jewish history, saw a great paradigm for the disruptive transition to modernity in the messianic upheavals of the seventeenth century and their radically antinomian aftermath. Neither man could conceive humanity making its way through the wilderness of existence without the guide of a metaphysical compass, for each assumed that what makes us human is our capacity to live in a community sharing wisdom, conscious of our relation to ultimate realities. Kafka's paradoxical authority for them lies in his ability to embrace without flinching the contradictions of this whole painful historical dislocation. He refuses to sever himself from the world of origins anchored in belief, but he is not for a moment deceived about its momentous decline. In his fiction he reenacts, transmogrified, the gestures of tradition in a kind of perverse reverence, without either spoofing tradition or being piously sentimental about it. From the center of dread he plucks the possibility of humor, and, as Benjamin intimated just before the end, hoping Scholem would see some analogue in the esoteric annals of Jewish mysticism, humor might yet become the funhouse mirror in which to glimpse one of the elusive faces of God. Perhaps Kafka himself, as he suggested more than once in his diaries and letters, was trying to achieve more than human imagination could do. Benjamin and Scholem, with their extraordinary minds, strained to catch the spiritual aim of that trying, which seems urgent enough a task to have undertaken as the world trembled under the shadow of destruction.

Kafka, Benjamin, and Scholem variously launched on a daring experiment in the recovery of Judaism under historical circumstances that made such an undertaking difficult, ambiguous, fraught with spiritual dangers, perhaps unfeasible. They shared a sense that the route of assimilation which their fathers had followed ultimately led to a dead end. They all perceived a sustaining power of visionary truth and an authenticity in Jewish tradition while fearing that this truth and this authenticity might no longer be accessible to them. Paradoxically, the very act of turning imaginatively toward a tradition receding into the past gave a depth of definition to the modernism of their respective literary enterprises as novelist, critic, and historian. In order to see the force of that paradox, we must consider in detail the intricacies of their relation to language, interpretation, tradition, and revelation.

TWO

ON NOT KNOWING
HEBREW

ℸℸℸ

In a dream I saw myself in Goethe's study . . . Goethe rose to his feet and accompanied me to an adjoining chamber, where a table was set for my relatives. It seemed prepared, however, for many more than their number. Doubtless there were places for my ancestors.

Walter Benjamin, *One-Way Street*

The horizon of Hebrew for the Jewish writer deeply assimilated in German intellectual culture can be marked, in the most literal sense, graphically: Hebrew is a language written in strange, forbidding square letters, against the grain of all European systems, from right to left. The historical attachment of Jews to the stubborn particularism of their own graphic system is mirrored in their practice of clinging to the Hebrew script even when they converted one of the surrounding languages into a distinctive Jewish language, as they did with Yiddish in Central and Eastern Europe. Hebrew loomed above all as a language of antithetical cultural alternatives for the assimilated writer pondering the prospect of reversing field of identity, and I doubt whether it could have served that psychological function so handily were it written in the familiar Latin script. In its own characters, at once daunting and appealing, it could exert the allure of the exotic, figuring visually as the alien other tongue that was also paradoxically the language of origins.

The leading Israeli poet, Yehuda Amichai, nicely catches this association of cultural character and script in the opening lines of his recent "Temporary Poem"—oddly enough, a poem triggered by the *intifada*:

> Hebrew and Arabic script go from east to west
> Latin script from west to east,
> Languages are like cats.
> One must not go against the direction of the fur.[1]

Amichai is, admittedly, a poet who delights in teasing out the metaphorical possibilities of all objects of contemplation, but my guess is that this particular perception occurs more readily to him as a native speaker of German (he emigrated to Palestine with his parents at the age of twelve) than it would to a native Israeli, for whom there is, at least to begin with, no linguistic alternative. Amichai's transposition of right and left into opposing points of the compass has the effect of raising the stakes of the game of inscription. Languages, that is, are seen to have a kind of geospiritual orientation. If we may extrapolate from this image a line of cultural history that bears directly on the subject of assimilation and Jewish identity, Hebrew moves from east to west, from the Bible and the Talmud created in the lands of Israel and Babylonia to the consciousness of Jews settled in the Rhineland and beyond, who in the course of time would absorb the surrounding language and culture. The languages written in Latin script, on the other hand, move from west to east (if one adopts the Israel-centered perspective of Amichai's poem and ignores the New World), following the twin paths of exploration and colonial conquest. This orientation, according to the logic of Amichai's second image, which is characteristically playful and self-deflating, reflects an intrinsic, organic, stubborn directionality of the language and the culture: like the fur of a cat, you must stroke it only in the direction it grows.

Kafka, Benjamin, and Scholem all became German writers. For the first two, Hebrew remained, in rather different ways, just what I called it at the outset: a horizon. Scholem, of course, propelled himself into the Hebrew world beyond the horizon but without severing as a writer his bonds with the German sphere. In an address to the Bavarian Academy of the Arts in Munich in 1974, he spoke of a long period of alienation from the German language and claimed, with some exaggeration, that for several decades after his emigration from Berlin to Jerusalem he worked primarily in Hebrew. It is true that many of the specialized monographs, scholarly articles, and textual editions that he produced from the 1920s through the 1940s were written in Hebrew, both for practical reasons and for other reasons that we will take up in due course. But in point of fact, the grand synthesis of his first two decades of scholarly activity, *Major Trends in Jewish Mysticism* (1941), was composed in German (and translated into English by George Lichtheim for its initial presentation as a series of lectures in New York and then for publication), as was his large-scale study, *Origins of the Kabbalah* (1962), though the latter was a development of a much shorter 1948 Hebrew version. Most of Scholem's influential essays of overview and interpretation were also written in German, and the only major work originally composed in Hebrew was his two-volume biography of Sabbatai Sevi—for reasons dictated by the subject that we will consider.

All three of our writers, then, including the Scholem who announced his estrangement from German, maintained a necessary and, one may say, loving relationship with their native language, but it was not untouched by an awareness of contradictions, especially in the case of Kafka and Scholem. These contradictions arise above all from a perception of the sons that their fathers' roots in German culture were shallow, and perhaps too recent to be anything but shallow. Hermann Kafka was born in a Bohemian *shtetl*, his first language was Czech (presumably with some Yiddish in the background), and he was never completely comfortable in the later-acquired German he would use through most of his adult life. Moving to Prague, he eventually became the prosperous owner of a dry-goods shop employing several salespeople. He had the energy and determination of a self-made man, according to Franz Kafka's testimony; but, as his son also stresses in *The Letter to His Father*, the self-making equally involved deracination. Arthur Scholem, the father of Gerhard, who would later Hebraize his name as Gershom, was the financially comfort-

able owner of a Berlin printshop he had inherited from his own
father, who had been raised in an Orthodox home and then
had broken with traditional observance. Emil Benjamin, Walter's father, was a wealthy antiquarian and art dealer in turn-of-
the-century Berlin. Of the three fathers, he represents the
upper end of the bourgeois scale, and Benjamin's reminis-
cences of his childhood reflect a sumptuousness of surround-
ings and an aesthetic richness beyond anything glimpsed in
the Kafka and Scholem households.

Scholem's oddly impassive memoir of his early years, *From
Berlin to Jerusalem*, which stands in sharp contrast to the lyric
impressionism of Benjamin's two collections of autobiographical fragments, nevertheless offers a fine illustrated catalogue of
the inner contradictions of the German-Jewish milieu in that
era. His grandfather's original name was Scholem Scholem. In
his later years, having become a Wagner enthusiast, he assumed the first name of Siegfried. On his tombstone, "Siegfried Scholem" was inscribed in Latin letters and "Scholem
Scholem" in Hebrew. Siegfried's son Arthur seems not to have
been given a Hebrew name, and, when he died in 1925,
"Arthur Scholem" alone was inscribed on his tombstone. (An
epitaph, it should be said, is no trivial matter, for it is, after all,
the last lapidary summation of who a person has been in his
earthly span—think of Stendhal's emphatic gesture of reiden-
tification in willing that his tombstone bear an Italian version
of his name, "Arrigo Beyle." We will have occasion to reflect
further on the presence of epitaphs in the imagination of
Kafka and Benjamin.) Scholem recalls in his autobiography
the Christmas of 1911, when he was fourteen: under the
family Christmas tree he found as a present a black-framed
portrait of Theodor Herzl, a gesture on the part of his parents
to accommodate his newfound interest in Zionism. This pro-
miscuous mingling of identities was too much for the young
Gerhard, and in subsequent years he made a point of staying
away from the house at Christmastime. The toleration of his

Zionism, at least by his father, would also prove fragile. On February 15, 1917, Arthur, finally fed up with the disloyalty to Germany he perceived in his son's Zionism, sent him a registered letter, addressed to his own house, giving Gerhard two weeks' notice to vacate the paternal premises and not to return without his father's express permission.[2] (Eventually there was a reconciliation.) Arthur Scholem made a great show of his staunch German identity and his freedom from petty parochialism, but his son wryly recalls that virtually everyone in the circle of his father's social acquaintances was a Jew.

One of the salient traits of the modern European intelligentsia, at least since the middle of the nineteenth century, has been its impetus to rebel against its own bourgeois origins. Sartre's massive biography of Flaubert, *The Family Idiot*, might be construed as the definitive stocktaking of this impetus, both because it elaborately records it, quite persuasively, in the career of Flaubert, and because it expresses so vehemently, for page after page after page, Sartre's own rage against all that seemed to him false and hateful and oppressive in the bourgeoisie. The cluster of characteristics that made the bourgeois fathers (and in most instances, not so much the mothers) odious—materialism, conformism, complacency, snobbery, stilted propriety, hardworking sobriety, belief in family, society, and progress—is familiar from the work of countless writers. The antibourgeois impulse is strong in Benjamin, Kafka, and Scholem, although in the case of the last two it was concentrated in the chthonic world they explored in their writing, while outwardly both preserved the forms of a bourgeois way of life. (Benjamin, by contrast, lived a life on the margins of society, but this might have turned out otherwise had his *Habilitation* dissertation been accepted and had he received a university appointment.) In the present connection, what I want to stress is that for all three—most signally for Kafka and Scholem—the rebellion against bourgeois origins, that quest for what Scholem called "radical solutions," was intimately associated with and dramatically reinforced by a rebellion against the complacency and superficiality of the parents' assimilationism. It is the essential respect in which the modern Jewish writer, because of the peculiarity of his ambiguous cultural location, becomes an extreme and exemplary instance of the modern writer in general.

Kafka is the most ruthless critic of the vapidness and the futility of the paternal project of assimilation. In *The Letter to His Father*, he reflects on the emptiness in Hermann Kafka's perfunctory preservation of a highly vestigial Judaism, and he entertains the fantasy that if only his father had remained anchored in traditional practice, they might have met on the common ground of Judaism. Kafka's most trenchant critique of what he saw as the ineluctable contradictions of assimilation occurs in a 1921 letter to Max Brod and is argued, instructively, on linguistic grounds. The passage has often been quoted, for good reason, but it is important to recall here as the text that provides the essential definition of the negative ground that actuated the quest for Hebrew. (Kafka, it should be observed, was deeply involved in the study of Hebrew at this late point in his life.) Speaking of the satirist Karl Kraus, Kafka stresses the role in Kraus's wit played by *mauscheln*—the use of Yiddish-German dialect. "This *mauscheln*," he writes to Brod "consists in a bumptious, tacit, or self-pitying appropriation of someone else's property, something not earned, but stolen by means of a relatively casual gesture." Going beyond even this harshness, Kafka proceeds to a generalization about German-Jewish writing that is surely one of the most unforgiving statements ever made about the ambiguous predicament of the Diaspora Jew writing in a Gentile language. Kafka mentions the recently fashionable oedipal complex of psychoanalytic doctrine (he was clearly one of its most accomplished connoisseurs) but says he prefers another version of father-son conflict, one that centers on "the father's Jewishness." His uncompromising description of the cultural consequences of this conflict is altogether disquieting:

> Most young Jews who began to write German wanted to leave Jewishness behind them, and their fathers approved of this, but vaguely (this vagueness was what was so outrageous to them). But with their posterior legs they were still glued to their fathers' Jewishness and with their waving anterior legs they found no new ground. The ensuing despair became their inspiration . . . The product of their despair could not be German literature, though outwardly it seemed to be so. They existed among three impossibilities, which I just happen to call linguistic impossibilities . . . These are: the impossibility of not writing, the impossibility of writing German, the impossibility of writing differently. One might also add a fourth impossibility, the impossibility of writing. . .[3]

The crushing truth of these strictures is obviously a truth of exaggeration, and Kafka in another frame of mind might not have put it so bleakly. In any case, intellectual work of the highest order exhibits a surprising capacity to surmount seeming impossibilities, and this all three of our figures achieved in becoming entirely authentic, entirely uncharacteristic German writers. Scholem made himself the master of a powerful scholarly German, ranging from dry precision and painstaking clarity in the exposition of technical intricacies to nuanced evocativeness in conjuring up psychological states, visions of God and man and history. But he used the fine-honed tools of German philology—primarily a method of investigation, but secondarily, at least for him, a form of prose as well—to explore the most un-German of subjects: the unknown and bizarre world of Jewish mysticism, embodied in a wealth of neglected texts composed in Aramaic and Hebrew, which for the most part had stood beyond the purview of German historical scholarship. Benjamin, as Hannah Arendt observed, took up a project analogous to Scholem's in choosing as the subject for his *Habilitation* the German Baroque *Trauerspiel*, a historically remote genre that in its bizarre extremeness and violence had seemed as marginal to German literature as the Kabbalah had seemed to Jewish history. Although he also devoted studies to the central figure of Goethe and to contemporaries such as Kafka and Karl Kraus and his friend Bertolt Brecht, and although he announced in his crucial letter to Scholem of January 20, 1930 (written in French!), that he aspired to be the leading critic of German literature, his major energies in his mature years were devoted to French writers from Baudelaire to Breton and Proust. The gnomic style he forged to express his critical vision was a curious compound of metaphysical abstraction and dense lyricism, by turns opaque and illuminating. It may have had certain odd antecedents in German literature since the eighteenth century, but it was distinctively his own peculiar prose, a way of writing authentic German from a marginal point of departure without committing the sin of *mauscheln*. Kafka, who explicitly stigmatized that sin and in his letter to Brod seemed to despair of avoiding it, hammered out a pellucid German, with the exacting style of Flaubert as his ideal, that perhaps drew on certain German countertraditional figures such as Kleist as prose models but in any case created the effect of a language weirdly severed from its historical roots. If he aspired as stylist to be a German Flaubert, one must imagine a Flaubert deliberately sealing off the background of Racine and Voltaire and Rousseau, making oblique use only of an occasional against-the-grain type such as Benjamin Constant. If one major aspect of modernist literature is to make the act of writing a ceremony of conspicuous estrangement—its outward tokens exile, rebellion, social alienation, and formal iconoclasm—Kafka, Benjamin, and Scholem, in at once incorporating and transcending the contradictions of their Jewish origins, became extreme and therefore exemplary instances of the modern writer.

But as the three pursued their variously idiosyncratic literary projects in German, Hebrew as the linguistic and cultural antipode entered into the imaginative world of each. The case of Scholem, at least on the surface, is the simplest because he precipitously plunged into Hebrew at an early age and remained immersed in it. On the occasion of his pro forma bar mitzvah, he was given a set of Heinrich Graetz's *History of the Jews,* and reading Graetz (who was also a catalyst in the adult Kafka's fascination with Judaism) kindled his interest in Judaism and its classical language. He began to study Hebrew, was soon devoting fifteen hours a week to it in addition to his regular *gymnasium* obligations. Endowed with the unfair advantage of a genius for language—in contrast to the mere facility exhibited by Benjamin and Kafka—by the age of sixteen he was studying the Talmud and by seventeen seems to have achieved a thorough mastery of all the strata of Hebrew, biblical, rabbinic, medieval, and modern. There were, of course, plain practical motives for his learning Hebrew. With his commitment to Zionism, he thought early on of emigration to Palestine after the completion of his formal studies, and Hebrew was the language he would have to use in his new country. Vocationally, after a flirtation with mathematics and philosophy, he became interested in the study of Jewish mysticism, for which a perfect control of Hebrew and its sister-language Aramaic was a prerequisite. (His first idea for a doctoral thesis was the kabbalistic conception of language.) But in this very period, he also laid heavy stress on Hebrew as the vehicle of return to a different spiritual world.

Thus, in Berne in 1919, where he was living in proximity to Walter and Dora Benjamin, he observed in a private notation (published posthumously): "thus we abandoned the language of our childhood and we began to study the language of youth imbued with endless resonance. We saw Hebrew then as the only way."[4] Still more revealingly, in a letter to the German-Jewish theologian Franz Rosenzweig on the occasion of Rosenzweig's fortieth birthday in 1926, Scholem perceived a kind of explosive spiritual danger in the revival of Hebrew as a vernacular: "People here actually do not realize what they are doing. They think they have turned Hebrew into a secular language, that they have pulled out its apocalyptic sting. But this is untrue. The secularization of a language is a mere phrase, no more than a slogan." In a letter to Scholem a year and a half earlier (May 20–25, 1925), Benjamin had puzzled over what Scholem could have meant by writing him that the revived language threatened to turn against those who spoke it. The letter to Rosenzweig provides the fullest response to this query by working out a kind of mythic plot in which the Hebrew language is imagined as a system of deep taps into the abyss—a key word throughout Scholem's writing—which, once having been activated, will open up an irresistible resurgence of the depths:

> A language is composed of names. The power of the language is bound up in the name, and its abyss is sealed within the name. Having conjured up the ancient names day after day, we can no longer suppress their potencies. We roused them, and they will manifest themselves, for we have conjured them up with very great power.[5]

The conception of language here is strikingly different from the strictly synchronic notion of an arbitrary system of signifiers that has been so influential from Saussure to poststructuralism. Language is seen as something steeped in the potent medium of historical experience—or perhaps one might even infer that there are attributes intrinsic to a particular language that *generate* historical experience. It never wholly surrenders what it has absorbed. On the contrary, the strong and distinctive perceptions of value, time and space, God and creation and history incarnated in the old words lie in wait, ready to spring out again, to make history happen anew, perhaps in unsettling ways. Hebrew *qets* points to the end of time and the end of all flesh in the Deluge story and the end of the familiar human order, unlike the German *Ende* or its equivalent in other European languages, which refers first of all to the flatter, more mundane scales of geometry and chronometry and mechanical process. One wonders whether Scholem regarded the stirring of apocalyptic currents in contemporary Zionism such as the Gush Emunim movement as a predictable unleashing of dangerous potentials implicit in the very revival of Hebrew. In any event, Hebrew as the language of overpowering revelation and spiritual abysses scared him and, self-proclaimed religious anarchist that he was, deeply attracted him as well. The antithesis of both *Muttersprache* and the bland bourgeois culture of the fathers, it was an *Ursprache* that provided access to a perilous and challenging realm as readily as, and perhaps more dependably than, the hashish with which Benjamin at one point experimented or the dreams that tormented Kafka.

If the return to Hebrew had this spiritual and experiential dimension, it also had an ideological motive that spoke clearly to Scholem and implicitly to Kafka, but not to Benjamin, who never moved far enough into a Jewish national perspective to be touched by such considerations. I have in mind not the obvious fact that Hebrew was the instrument of political Zionism as a nationalist revival but, more in keeping with our focus on intellectual identity and historical consciousness, the power of Hebrew as the indigenous Jewish language to liberate those who used it from any constraining awareness of what the Gentiles might think. Some Zionists have provocatively argued that anything written about the Jews in a Western language is inevitably apologetic, and there may be a kernel of truth in the exaggeration. Scholem, writing to Benjamin on December 18, 1935, tells him of a long essay he is working on that he is sure would be of great interest to his friend, but he explains that it "can only be written in Hebrew anyway, at least if the author is to remain free from apologetic inhibitions." The essay appeared the following year in a Hebrew annual under the title "Mitsvah haba'ah ba'averah," and only in 1971 in English translation as "Redemption through Sin."[6] The essay would certainly have been of compelling interest to Benjamin, and it in fact marked a watershed in Scholem's career. It was his first major statement about the great Sabbatian heresy, his first long look into that central abyss of Jewish history in which he saw a paradoxical mingling of antinomian, nihilistic forces of destruction and vital powers of national renewal. It would not have been easy to contemplate all this in German.

The very title is a shocking and untranslatable Sabbatian pun on an indigenous Hebrew concept. In the Talmud, a *mitsvah*, or the performance of a divine commandment, that, literally, "comes through transgression" is a legal notion: what, for example, is the legal status of a *sukkah*, the biblically enjoined festival booth, built with stolen materials? In the Sabbatian antinomian redefinition, the *mitsvah* comes through transgression because willfully committing the transgression—sexual, ritual, or whatever—is now seen as a paradoxical fulfillment of the divine precept. The use of Hebrew not only freed Scholem to handle this material without inhibition but also, as the instance of his title suggests, enabled him to work easily with a complex of concepts distinctively articulated in Jewish tradition that is almost too cumbersome to explain in another language. The program he laid out in "Redemption through Sin" was realized on a grand scale in his 1956 biography of Sabbatai Sevi, also composed in Hebrew.

Kafka tried to make his way toward Hebrew at about the same time he became aware that his life was beginning to ebb—a synchronicity that may not have been accidental. His first great surge of interest in Judaism and Jewish culture had occurred in the fall of 1911, when he was twenty-eight, with the arrival in Prague of a Yiddish theatrical troupe. Kafka was mesmerized by the group, spent evening after evening watching its performances, became infatuated with one of the actresses and a close friend of the leading actor. Within a few weeks, he was reading Graetz, then Meyer Isser Pines's *Histoire de la littérature Judéo-Allemande*. His diaries in this period are studded with references to the Yiddish performances, to the world of folklore and religious practice represented in the plays, to bits of talmudic and Hasidic lore he had culled from his reading. Kafka also manifested a growing interest in Zionism, which like all the important interests in his life was oscillating and ambivalent. He began studying Hebrew in the late spring or early summer of 1917, on his own and with the aid of tutors. (His first tutor was Dr. Friedrich Thieberger, a learned young man who was the son of a Prague rabbi.)[7] In early August 1917 he experienced his first lung hemorrhage, which was diagnosed a month later as tuberculosis: the disease would kill him within six years, at the age of forty-one.

From this point onward, as his failing health compelled him to take repeated sick leaves and to spend time at various sanitaria, his correspondence attests to his persistent involvement with Hebrew. In a letter of September 27, 1918, he chides Max Brod for making errors in a Hebrew letter he had sent to Kafka but commends him for his general effort. On April 8, 1920, he announces that he has been able to eke out a Hebrew conversation with a Turkish-Jewish rug dealer he met at Meran. (It remains unclear what level of conversational fluency in Hebrew Kafka ever attained. Georg Langer, a secular Prague Jew who for a while converted to Hasidism and wrote a book called *Die Erotik der Kabbala*, later remembered having conversations with his friend Kafka exclusively in Hebrew, but it is hard to assess the accuracy of this recollection.) In July 1923 he expresses gratification to Hugo Bergmann at having received from his old classmate his first Hebrew letter from Palestine. (In a curious crossover of destinies, a decade later Bergmann would become the lover, then the second husband of Scholem's first wife, Escha.) Also in the summer of 1923, Kafka reads Hebrew together with Dora Dyamant, the young woman of East European Hasidic background who was his last love. Through 1923, the last complete year of his life, he says he is able to read little, but most of it is Hebrew. In a postcard to Robert Klopstock sent from Berlin on October 25, 1923, he writes that he has been working his way through Y. H. Brenner's Hebrew novel *Shekhol ve-Kishalon*, a page a day. "It is difficult for me in every respect, and not very good."[8] The novel, whose title has been rendered in English as *Breakdown and Bereavement*, had appeared in Hebrew just five years earlier. The difficulty Kafka refers to is primarily linguistic but perhaps also emotional, for if he had thought to discover some vista of hope in this modern Hebrew work, it revealed to him instead a landscape of despair and frustration, for all its Jerusalem setting, eerily akin to the one that was his constant companion. On artistic grounds, he could not have thought it very good; Brenner's ragged, at times seemingly amorphous prose, his loose handling of plot and scene, were the antithesis of Kafka's ideal of exacting form. Kafka continued to puzzle over the pointed spoonerism of Brenner's title. In a postscript to a letter to Klopstock written in early November, he observes: "*Shekhol ve-Kishalon* are two nouns I do not fully understand. At any rate they are an attempt to set down the quintessence of misfortune. *Shekhol* means literally childlessness, so perhaps unfruitfulness, fruitlessness, pointless effort; and *Kishalon* means literally: stumble, fall."[9] He was right etymologically about *Kishalon*, which however has the more extended sense of "failure," but revealingly wrong about *Shekhol*, which actually means "bereavement through the death of a child," a state he could not quite conceive because he could not imagine for himself the preceding condition of being a father. His transposition of the term into his own predicament of childlessness, pointless effort is a linguistic error, but it is faithful enough to the bleak reality of Brenner's fictional world.

Although Kafka was physically present in Berlin several times when Benjamin and Scholem were in the city, their paths never crossed. There is, however, one instructive reference by

Kafka to Scholem in a letter to his fiancée, Felice Bauer (September 22, 1916), which Scholem later was delighted to discover when the correspondence was published. Felice had attended a lecture at the Berlin Jewish community center by Siegfried Lehmann, who presented a program for Jewish education that Scholem thought entirely muddled and pretentious. Scholem responded in the discussion period with the most vehement objection: "I demanded that people learn Hebrew and go to the sources instead of occupying themselves with such literary twaddle."[10] Felice Bauer reported this exchange to Kafka, and he commented on it in the following terms: "theoretically I am always inclined to favor proposals such as those made by Herr Scholem, which demand the utmost, and by so doing achieve nothing. So one simply musn't appraise such proposals and their value by the actual result laid before one . . . Actually, Scholem's proposals in themselves are not impracticable."[11]

The paradoxical formulation is characteristic of Kafka. There is, he suggests, an intrinsic value of truth, or authenticity, that justifies the Hebraist proposal—or, indeed, any proposal whatever—quite apart from the practical issue of its feasability. And again, perhaps the unfeasible might prove perfectly feasible (a principle without which Zionism and the revival of Hebrew would never have been accomplished). Such thinking about demands of the linguistic utmost must surely have come into play a year later when Kafka began to devote himself to the study of Hebrew as the first clear signs of his terminal illness were manifesting themselves.

Why, in fact, was he studying Hebrew under the shadow of death during this period when he was writing stories such as "The Hunter Gracchus," "An Old Manuscript," "A Report to the Academy," and "Investigations of a Dog"—all of them fictions with a surface universality founded on a Jewish thematic matrix—and struggling with his last novel, *The Castle*, to be left unfinished like its two predecessors? His friends Bergmann and Brod tried to encourage him to consider emigration to Palestine. The prospect intermittently attracted him, but he knew he would never attain it, just as he would never be able to marry (he sometimes seemed to draw an analogy between the two unrealizable consummations). Near the end, he said he would be content to live in any clement southern region, devoting himself to Hebrew.

Although Kafka himself does not offer explicit motives, the direct evidence of the letters and diaries and the oblique evidence of the fiction suggest that what drew him to Hebrew was similar to what drew Scholem. Here was a language that reached back to a world in every respect antithetical to the realm of Hermann Kafka's shop and bourgeois apartment and his thin veneer of Prague German. Whether or not Kafka the writer of fiction was a heretical kabbalist, as Scholem insisted, he was desperately concerned with the idea of revelation and the human effort to relate to a realm of the transcendent, and as a Jew he saw Hebrew as the primary, powerful medium, the *Ursprache*, of these concerns. In a postcard to Felice Bauer dated September 16, 1916, he speaks of "the dark complexity of Judaism, which contains so many impenetrable features," a notion entirely consonant with Scholem's perception of a perilous abyss embodied in Hebrew. To follow the original words of the creation story, the Psalms, the prophecies of Isaiah; to make a first tentative foray into the dialectical labyrinth of the Talmud; to ponder the modern literary articulation of the millennia-old language—all this could provide neither intellectual solutions nor spiritual redemption for the dying Kafka, but it did put him in touch with something he could feel was authentic. In the absence of hope, he settled for truth, a truth of historical identity in which his people had narratively imagined, legally defined, questioned and quarreled about its role in the world and its relationship with God.

Of our three writers, Benjamin is the one who kept Hebrew strictly as a horizon. Depending on one's point of view or on what point in his life one is considering, the puzzlement is why he persisted in not knowing Hebrew or, on the contrary, why he wanted to know Hebrew at all. It is unlikely that the direction of Hebrew would have ever occurred to him had it not been for his friendship with Scholem, which began in 1915, when Benjamin was twenty-three. Much later, in a letter following the painful one in which Benjamin had renounced his plans for coming to Palestine, he attested to the fact that all his interest in Judaism had been through the medium of his friend Gerhard. (Some recent Benjamin scholars have pointed to evidence of an interest in Judaism before he met Scholem, but, at least in his own perception, it was through the influence of his younger friend that he came to an encounter with Judaism.) The friendship became progressively intense in the last couple of years of the Great War and during the subsequent three or four years. Benjamin first undertakes the study of Hebrew in 1920 but abandons it after a few months. Five years later (May 20–25, 1925), writing to Scholem, who has been living in Jerusalem for two years, he announces his turn toward Marxism and speaks of his intention to make a trip to Moscow and also, "even if only incidentally," to join the Communist Party (he never did). But Moscow is seen as a polar alternative to Jerusalem, and at this point he has by no means given up on the latter: the two, indeed, are different radical routes away from the German bourgeois realm of origins which he had to escape at all costs. He finds himself, he tells Scholem, in "a frightening conflict of forces (my personal forces) in which both this [Moscow, the Party] and the study of Hebrew necessarily partake."

Two years later, in the summer of 1927, on the occasion of the first of their two reunions after Scholem's emigration, Benjamin, having spent two months in Moscow the previous year, moved as close to the Jerusalem pole as he would ever come. The long hours the two men spent together in Paris involved, according to Scholem's testimony, fierce debates about Marxism but also included a surprising expression of adherence to the goal of Hebrew. Scholem introduced Benjamin to Judah Magnes, chancellor of the Hebrew University, who was then also passing through Paris, and in a three-way conversation Benjamin, according to Scholem's recollection, ardently affirmed that "his focal point would lie for him in an occupation with the Hebrew language and literature," that "he thought he would be able to reach an entirely new level only as a critic of Hebrew texts."[12] There was talk of Benjamin's assuming a faculty position in a new school of humanities at the Hebrew University, and, after Magnes returned to Jerusalem, he arranged for a monthly stipend to be paid to Benjamin in order to free him sufficiently from his journalistic labors so that he could devote himself to the study of Hebrew. On June 26, 1929, Benjamin writes Hugo von Hofmannsthal, the playwright, poet, and editor, that he has been hard at work on Hebrew for two months and plans to leave for Jerusalem in September where he will concentrate exclusively on the study of the language. He reminds Hofmannsthal that on their first meeting the Austrian poet, himself half-Jewish, had forcefully told Benjamin that the lack of Hebrew was "a great gap in my [Benjamin's] life that was equally visible and striking."

But within a few months the whole Hebrew project was definitively abandoned. In the end, Moscow was not the pole that drew Benjamin away from Jerusalem—although he remained an idiosyncratic Marxist for another decade—but rather Paris. The letter to Scholem of January 20, 1930, in which he renounces his Hebrew plans is written in French, according to his own explanation, because French can serve him as "a sort of alibi," enabling him to say to his friend things that would be hard to say in the intimacy of their native tongue. But I think there is a second motive for the choice of French, which is that it is the linguistic token of his at last firmly elected vocation. Hebrew also had been associated with vocation, with the idea of becoming, as he confided to Scholem, a kind of latter-day Rashi or ibn Ezra, an exegete of sacred texts. French was neither *Muttersprache* nor *Ursprache* but *la langue de la civilisation européenne*, which would be his great subject. Although in the letter he says he aspires to be the leading critic of German literature, the major project he mentions, which both holds him in Europe and leaves him no leisure for Hebrew, is his book, *Parisian Arcades*. The title he later settled on for this never-completed undertaking—*Paris, Capital of the Nineteenth Century*—is especially revelatory about his geospiritual orientation as a European (not a German), writing from west to east. The title of course points up his concern with the palpable medium of history—in the extant fragments, he evokes it with a kind of *Marxisant* lyric impressionism—but it also reflects a desire to displace national geography into temporality. In the ideal realm of his project, Paris is the capital not of France but of a century, and he comes to it not as a marginal German (soon to be forced into permanent exile) but as a European, beyond the constraints of merely national perspectives, heir to the culture of that extraordinary century of transition. Toward the end of the decade, as the inevitability of war became ominously clear, Benjamin would not move to extricate himself from Paris until it was too late because his project was there and his project was, virtually in the theological sense of the term, his vocation.[13]

What remains of Hebrew in Benjamin's literary work—especially but not exclusively in his earlier metaphysical phase—is a very peculiar idea of language. He could not, like Scholem, stress the way language was pregnant with the forces of its own age-old history because he had not actually entered into the historical secrets of the ancient language. Instead, he took from the Kabbalah—which he knew through his discussions with Scholem and through German scholarly and speculative writing on the subject—the notion of language as cosmogonic agency, as both the ultimate constituent of creation and the key to understanding it. (I am not sure whether Scholem himself actually believed in this idea, though he devoted many pages to explaining its various articulations in kabbalistic doctrine.) Thus, Benjamin comes to a transnational, ahistorical notion of "language as such" (*Sprache überhaupt*), first spelled out in his essay "On Language as Such and the Language of Man," a piece initially drafted in 1916 after his early conversations with Scholem on the theory of language in Jewish mysticism. The conception of language, which also informs his perplexing essay of 1923, "The Task of the Translator," is frankly mystical. Before any particular historical declension of language there is an ideal, divine language—much as Hebrew figures in rabbinic interpretation. Benjamin's own analysis broadly follows the Bible, he affirms, "in presupposing language as an ultimate reality, perceptible only in its manifestation, inexplicable and mystical." Language transcends any mundane function of communication in human culture, "for the whole of nature, too, is imbued with a nameless, unspoken language, the residue of the creative word of God, which is perceived in man as the cognizing name and above man as the judgment suspended over him."[14] Although it has become fashionable to cite and celebrate Benjamin's most vatic pronouncements as his greatest profundities, I frankly don't know what to make of this, however arresting it may be as a poetic image, and I am inclined to see it as the evocative, ultimately incoherent extravagance of a lyric literary imagination conjuring with mystical ideas. To put this somewhat differently, Benjamin's theory of language is Hebrew as conceived by the Kabbalah transposed into a universalized metaphysical abstraction, and precisely that transposition is the source of the strain on credence. Such speculation on the part of a German-Jewish writer is another path out of Kafka's terrible dilemma of the three linguistic impossibilities, but not, I think, a very persuasive path. If Benjamin ever fully escaped the anxiety of not knowing Hebrew, it was, as we shall see momentarily, in the realm of dreams.

In September 1939, after the Nazi occupation, Benjamin was taken to a "volunteer labor camp" at Clos St. Joseph Nevers, where he was detained for almost two months. All his letters from the camp, like most of his letters under the occupation, were written in French, presumably in order not to attract any extra attention from the censor. But one of these letters, to Gretel Adorno on October 10, 1939, has, as he observes at the beginning, a "double reason" for having been written in French, for it is devoted to recounting a dream that culminates in an enigmatic sentence pronounced in French. (Benjamin had become a good friend of Gretel Karplus Adorno ten years earlier. By 1939, she was living in New York with her husband, Theodor Adorno, the leading theorist of the Institute for Social Research.) The move from one language to another, and from one system of inscription to another, which has concerned us all along, is paramount in Benjamin's dream.

At the beginning of his letter Benjamin emphasizes that the dream, which came to him as he slept on his detention-camp pallet, was so extraordinarily beautiful that he felt compelled to share it, and at the end he says he awoke from it in a state of euphoria. It will be instructive to ponder the source of this euphoria. In the dream, Benjamin goes off with a certain Dr. Dausse, a physician friend who had once treated him for malaria. They find themselves in a ditch or excavation (*fouille*) surrounded by strange stone coffins arranged in pairs that have the inviting softness of beds. But just as they are about to stretch out in two of them, they realize that the coffin-beds are already occupied, and so, putting behind them this odd site where sleep and death and the—implicitly—erotic are joined, they go on their way, traversing a kind of forest. They soon come to a terrace fashioned out of boards on which they meet a group of women who seem somehow to belong to Dausse. Several of them strike the dreamer as remarkably beautiful. He takes off his panama hat, "which I inherited from

my father," and he is startled to see that there is a large crack across the top, with traces of red along the edges of the crack. This brings us to the crucial moment of the dream.

One of the ladies meanwhile had begun to perform handwriting analysis. I saw that she was holding something that had been written by me and that Dausse had given her. I was a little anxious about this expertise, fearing that certain of my intimate characteristics might thus be revealed. I approached. What I saw was a cloth covered with images, the only graphic elements of which I could make out were the top parts of the letter *d*, the tapering lengths of which revealed an extreme aspiration toward spirituality. This part of the letter was besides furnished with a little blue-bordered veil, and the veil swelled against the drawing as though it were in a breeze. That was the only thing I could "read"—the rest presented indistinct patterns of waves and clouds. The conversation for a moment centered on this writing. I do not remember the opinions stated; in compensation, I know quite well that at a given moment I said verbatim the following: "It is a question of changing a piece of poetry into a scarf." (Es handelte sich darum, aus einem Gedicht ein Halstuch zu machen.) I had scarcely uttered these words when something fascinating happened. I noticed that among the women there was one, very beautiful, who had lain down in a bed. Awaiting my explanation, she made a movement quick as lightning. It took less than a second for her to perform this gesture. She parted a tiny end of the cover that enveloped her in her bed. And it was not in order to let me see her body but to let me see the outline of the sheet, which was meant to offer imagery analogous to that which I must have "written," many years ago, as a gift for Dausse. I knew quite well that the lady had made that movement.[15]

I have no pretensions to psychoanalyze Benjamin, but the conjunction here of the erotic and the scriptorial is directly related to our concern with cultural identity and the triple impossibilities of writing. The odd superimposition of eros and death, a *Liebestod* that seems more *Liebe* than *Tod*, may well

reflect Benjamin's vision of suicide as escape, which he had long contemplated and which he would carry out in less than a year. This would explain in part the sense of euphoria after the dream. I refer especially to the coffins that are also beds, perhaps occupied by pairs of lovers, and that surface again as the bed with the beautiful woman, which now no longer has the outward appearance of a coffin. The panama hat with the crack across the top, inherited from Benjamin's father, betrays first of all a certain sense of social embarrassment, and it should be said that the dreamer feels himself to be something of an outsider to the group he has encountered on the terrace. This token of the debonair sophisticate, at home in fashionable society (as Emil Benjamin surely was), which has been passed on to the son, is suddenly seen in a state of terrible dilapidation. What is more, the hat is disfigured—or perhaps we should say transfigured, from the realm of the sartorial and the social to the asocial realm of the instinctual—by a fissure that is a strong image of female sexuality, the red-bordered crack (*fente*).

At this point in the dream, writing intervenes strangely and proves to be the means of moving successfully from the uneasy social sphere associated with the father to the private sphere of eros. The dreamer is afraid that the lady performing handwriting analysis (*graphologie*, in which Benjamin himself was expert) will discover things about him that he would prefer to keep secret—the tension between the desire to expose and the need to conceal that most writers feel, and perhaps German-Jewish writers more than most. However, all that can be seen of his writing is the tops of the *d*'s (of course, handwritten *d*'s), which aspire upward toward spirituality according to the graphological analysis, as Benjamin's own literary work repeatedly did. The *d* may be triggered by the proximity of Dausse, but it is also the initial character of the pseudonym Detlef, with which Benjamin signed his letters to Gretel Adorno, and so it is a personal signature. One wonders, since systems of inscription are at issue in this French dream that contains a German sentence, whether the overdetermined *d* also obliquely invokes *Deutsch*, the writer's point of departure and habitual medium. In any case, the writing here has been executed in the strange medium of cloth, and the metonymic links between cloth and the female body are strongly forged by the dream logic. Writing is transformed into a kind of embroidery, an activity associated with women, and the visible fragments of the letter *d* are outfitted with a little blue-bordered veil. At the crucial point of revelation, Benjamin recites the enigmatic sentence, "It is a question of changing a piece of poetry into a scarf [*fichu*]," and though he has already stressed that these words were pronounced in French, as if to make sure that Gretel Adorno will unswervingly understand them verbatim he translates them into German: *Es handelte sich darum, aus einem Gedicht ein Halstuch zu machen*. The *fichu/Halstuch* is a piece of cloth worn around a woman's neck, literally tied to the desired body. The enigma of the recited sentence embodies a utopian vision of language transformed into pure realized desire—a vision, incidentally, that would have made perfect sense to some of the radically antinomian offshoots of Scholem's Sabbatians. The word becomes body, or at least the stuff that touches the body. Beyond all the tensions and the rasping frictions of cultural difference, the act of inscription is neither German nor French nor Hebrew but pure materiality, showing in its form an aspiration to spirituality (down to up rather than left to right) but carrying the dreamer directly, as though language's walls of mediation had dissolved, to the beckoning bed of lovely carnality.

The teasing character of that concluding image of the woman in bed is noteworthy. If this were a piece of conscious literary invention rather than the account of a dream, a contemporary critic could easily claim that the issue of concealment and revelation was explicitly "thematized" here. The dreamer senses that the lightning gesture of the recumbent beauty is intended to expose not her body but rather a design in the sheet clinging to her body, *une imagerie,* which somehow corresponds to the embroidered, largely hidden image-writing on the mysterious cloth. Nevertheless, the evocation of this moment has a powerfully voyeuristic feel, as though it were more than patterns in cloth that the dreamer beheld. The woman provocatively pulls back a corner of the cover in the sort of sudden movement that would be used to offer an enticing glimpse of what is usually hidden. She is, moreover, a beautiful woman in bed, holding out some indefinable mystery to the male observer, who sees her, so he tells us in the sentence after the ones quoted above, not with his eyes but with "a kind of supplementary vision." Benjamin experiences this voyeuristic moment, which one might presume to be merely tantalizing, as a wonderful consummation: he emerges from the dream with a strong feeling of happiness that keeps him awake for hours, and he wants to share that feeling by describing it in a letter—again, a fusion of euphoria and writing—to Gretel Adorno.

Whatever all this may suggest about Benjamin's psychosexual life, it is a revealing manifestation of the problematic of language, writing, and experience that was the very matrix of his thinking. I would propose as the point of origin for his thought about language a sense of disquieting differences following from the condition of linguistic and cultural multiplicity. There is at least a residual sense of difference—a trace of Kafka's impossibilities—between himself, writing passionate and brilliant and intricate German, and other users of German, who as non-Jews may have another relation to the culture. There is the perplexing difference between one European language and the next, which leads him repeatedly to ponder the enigmas of translation and to imagine a divine language of cosmic universality that is somehow invoked in the linguistic transfer of the act of translation. And there is the fundamental difference between primal Hebrew, to which he

aspires but which he cannot bring himself to learn, and all the
languages written from left to right. In the dream he dreamt
toward the end of his life, all these differences melt away.
French and German seem to converge, perhaps become inter-
changeable. More evidently, writing ceases to be an unwitting
exposure of intimate personal traits or, like the panama hat, of
patrimony but becomes instead a sensuously concrete "imagery" free of the particularism of formal systems of script,
preserving only the tops of those d's as the vestiges of any
alphabet. The upwardly aspiring *d*s are also the sole residual
trace of Benjamin's concept of a divine language, while the
writing in cloth is no longer transcription or representation or
abstraction but realization of desire. The beautiful woman in
bed does not need to expose her nakedness or do anything
carnal with or for the dreamer: showing him the pattern in the
bed linens is enough because it is, after all, his own writing, a
self-expression at once significant and safely indecipherable,
which envelops her body. Outside the realm of dreams, writing is a haunting symptom of the dilemmas of cultural existence after Babel. No writer was more acutely aware of these
dilemmas and the impasses to which they could lead than
Kafka, on whom Benjamin long meditated, and who himself
was bemused by the myth of Babel. The Kabbalah in its own
way sought to transcend the dilemmas by conceiving the
written forms of primal Hebrew as keys to all cosmic mys-
teries. It is only the oneiric imagination of Benjamin that
glimpses another way out in the fantasy of a writing liberated
from all cultural codes that inscribes, in Blake's phrase, the
lineaments of gratified desire.

Of our three writers, the role of languages and Hebrew in the
work of Kafka is the most curious. Scholem's writing, of course,
constantly reflects his immersion in the world of Hebrew as
philologist, historian, and speculative thinker about language.
Benjamin's work occasionally makes explicit use of his musings
on the language and tradition he never actually learned, as in

his late essay on Kafka and in "Language as Such and the Language of Man." Kafka, on the other hand, despite his preoccupation with questions of Judaism and Jewish culture from 1911 onward and despite his sustained effort to learn Hebrew in the last six years of his life, rigorously excludes from his fiction all references to anything Jewish, with the exception of one story, "The Animal in the Synagogue," involving a strange beast in the women's gallery of a synagogue. Nothing on the surface of the novels and stories betrays the fact that the writer was a Jew. The characters never have distinctively Jewish names; the settings and institutions are modern urban and bureaucratic, like the bank and law courts and claustral apartments of *The Trial*; or archetypal, like the town and the Castle or the Chinese imperial realm; or fantastic, like *Amerika* and many of the stories and animal fables; or occasionally Christian, like the cathedral in *The Trial*. There is no question, I think of Kafka's trying to escape from or conceal his Jewish origins. What he sought to do instead—and this is arguably a chief source of the strange power of his work—was to convert the distinctive quandaries of Jewish existence into images of the existential dilemmas of mankind *überhaupt*, "as such." Perhaps he sensed that the way for him to overcome the danger, as a writer who felt himself in one crucial respect to be an outsider to German culture, of a "tacit . . . appropriation of someone else's property" was to make his own property German, and universally human as well. Although not every reader will agree with all the identifications of Jewish themes proposed by Kafka's many critics, his stories and novels are repeatedly and variously concerned with questions such as exile, assimilation, endangered community, revelation, commentary, law, tradition, and commandment. These themes are often made to reflect the neurotic obsessions that tormented Kafka, but not necessarily with a diminution of their universal implications; and sometimes Kafka articulates them as general reflections on culture and theology, especially in the shorter pieces.

In regard to language, the fiction carries out through the vehicle of German an unsparing critique of all illusions about the efficacy of language, including notions of a divinely given *Ursprache* that might offer humanity sure grounding in reality. The last story Kafka wrote, "Josephine the Singer, or the Mouse Folk," provides a particularly sharp satiric reduction of such illusions. The story deals explicitly with the tension and symbiosis between artist and audience, but, as numerous commentators have noted, it also has strong Jewish thematic resonances of the sort I have just proposed. The mouse folk, leading as it does a constantly precarious existence, often in need of consolation, collectively childish yet prematurely old, haunted by a tradition of singing ("in the old days our people did sing") though fallen into an era of unmusicality, presents a whole series of correspondences to the Jewish people in its Diaspora history. Because of the analogy intimated between the real singing of the old days and the grandeur of biblical Israel, the narrator's exposure of the true nature of Josephine's singing is not just a questioning of the possibility of sublime art but also a critique of the idea of transcendent language (Benjamin's or the Kabbalah's notion of Hebrew). The members of the mouse folk communicate with each other through a pathetic thin piping, and the effect of Josephine's art is achieved, so to speak, through a trick of acoustic mirrors: she, too, only pipes, for that is all the language that the mouse folk possesses.

The critique of claims made for language is carried back to the biblical record itself in "The City Coat of Arms," a one-page fable that is a more subversive rewriting of the story of the Tower of Babel than meets the casual eye. The tale in Genesis is one of the great etiological myths of the primeval age. Kafka's version displaces the primeval into the historical and thus fundamentally alters its meaning. He begins in the following matter-of-fact manner: "At first all the arrangements for building the Tower of Babel were characterized by fairly good order, indeed the order was perhaps too perfect, too much thought given to guides, interpreters, accommodations for the workmen, and roads of communication, as if there were centuries before one to do the work in."[16]

The narrator's businesslike informative tone and the rapid catalogue of instances of "order" almost rush us past the one item in the series that changes everything in the biblical story: *Dolmetscher*, interpreters. Unlike Genesis, where the tale begins when "the whole earth was of one language and of one speech," there is no primal universal language here, no aboriginal Hebrew through which God spoke the world and mankind into being. The multiplicity of languages is not the punishment and the instrument for frustrating the overweening ambition of the tower-builders, as in Genesis, but an assumed detail of their condition as men living in history. The crippling disunity that prevents the tower from rising toward its goal is a consequence of the inherent divisiveness of human nature, and the given multiplicity of tongues might inferrably be a result of this very divisiveness. Confident that the future progress of technology will make their project more easily achievable, the builders concentrate not on the tower but on the construction of a city for the workmen, and territorial disputes over neighborhoods and quarters soon lead to bloody conflict among the nationalities. The tower thus remains unbuilt, even comes to seem a pointless idea to later generations, who nevertheless remain enmired in the city. (The antiurbanism of Kafka's version is the one respect in which it is wholly consonant with the biblical original.) The narrator's conclusion introduces a startling perspective on the future of the city. Its coat of arms is a closed fist because "All the legends and songs that come to birth in that city are filled with longing for a prophesied day when the city would be destroyed by five successive blows from a gigantic fist."[17] There is no primal language to dream back to, no ideal of original unity to which to return. History in all its internecine strife becomes a trap

from which there is no escape—except through the intervention of apocalyptic destruction, which will provide relief, not
redemption, by putting an end to it all.

A negative solution on the individual level to the anguish of
entrapment in a world without hope of redemption is spelled
out in a fragment entitled "A Dream," which was evidently
composed for *The Trial* but then conflicted with the conclusion
of the novel that Kafka devised. Here again, the problematic
of language is associated with the idea of death as release, and,
as in Benjamin's actual dream, language is invoked as alphabetic inscription. Joseph K., the protagonist of *The Trial*, dreams
that he has gone on a walk that quickly leads him to a
cemetery. There he finds a freshly heaped grave mound that
exerts a strange fascination over him. Two men appear and
install a blank tombstone. Then an artist pops onto the scene.
Equipped with what looks like an ordinary pencil, he reaches
up to the tombstone and begins an inscription:

> . . . he wrote: HERE LIES—Every letter was clear and beautifully
> made, deeply incised and of the purest gold. When he had
> inscribed these two words he looked at K. over his shoulder; K.,
> who was very eager to know how the inscription would go, paid
> hardly any attention to the man but was intent only on the stone.
> And in fact the man turned again to continue writing, but he
> could not go on, something was hindering him, he let the pencil
> sink and once more turned toward K. This time K. looked back at
> him and noted that he was deeply embarrassed and yet unable to
> explain himself. All his earlier vivacity had vanished. That made
> K. feel embarrassed too; they exchanged helpless glances; there
> was some dreadful misunderstanding between them which nei-
> ther could resolve. An untimely little bell now began to ring from
> the cemetery chapel, but the artist made a sign with uplifted hand
> and the bell stopped. In a little while it began again; this time
> quite softly and without any insistence, breaking off again at
> once; as if it were only testing its own tone. K. felt miserable
> because of the artist's predicament, he began to cry and sobbed

for a long time into his cupped hands. The artist waited until K. had calmed down and then decided, since there was no help for it, just to go on with the inscription. The first small stroke that he made was a relief to K., but the artist obviously achieved it only with the greatest reluctance; the work, too, was no longer beautifully finished, above all there seemed to be a lack of gold leaf, pale and uncertain the stroke straggled down, only it turned into a very big letter. It was a J, it was almost finished, and at that moment the artist stamped angrily on the grave mound with one foot so that the soil all around flew up in the air. At long last K. understood him; it was too late to start apologizing now; with all his fingers he dug into the earth which offered almost no resistance; everything seemed prepared beforehand; a thin crust of earth had been constructed only for the look of the thing; immediately beneath it a great hole opened out, with steep sides, into which K. sank, wafted onto his back by a gentle current. And while he was already being received into impenetrable depths, his head still straining upwards on his neck, his own name raced upon the stone above him in great flourishes.

Enchanted by the sight, he woke up.[18]

Kafka's systematic transposition of his own keenly felt Jewish experience into a universal and hence marginally Christian vehicle is strikingly evident here. As in the novel, Joseph K.'s religious or ethnic identity is left rather vague, but the cemetery with its bell-ringing chapel must be Christian. Characteristically, however, the incidental detail of Christian setting is exploited not for its distinctively Christian nature but, on the contrary, for its archetypal resonance: Joseph K. need not seek to know for whom the bell tolls—it tolls for him. The cross-purposes at which K. and the artist find themselves are the quintessential Kafkan moment, the ground of virtually every Kafka plot: "there was some dreadful misunderstanding between them which neither could resolve." Had K. been simply willing to submit to his—sacrificial?—role in a prearranged scheme of inexorable justice, the mortuary artist could have gone on to execute the magic of his art in splendidly beautiful letters of the purest gold. As it is, given the disparity between the traditional artist and his recalcitrant, doggedly individual subject, the harmony of calligraphic art breaks down, leaving shaky, uneven strokes, bare of gold adornment—perhaps a wry image of Kafka's own modernist writing.

Let us ponder the cultural ramifications of the dream's peculiar focus on the inscription of letters. The first words K. sees, presumably incised toward the top of the tombstone, are *Hier ruht*, "Here lies." The displacement toward the universal in Kafka of which I have spoken is manifested here, in the strictest sense of the term, on the literal level. That displacement is in no way spelled out in the thematic structure of the story, but the pressure it exerts in the consciousness of the writer is far from negligible. I refer to the fact that for Kafka, oriented toward the horizon of Hebrew, and with a personal familiarity with graveyards that must have begun with the Jewish cemetery of Prague, behind *Hier ruht*, read from left to right, lie two Hebrew letters, *peh nun*, read from right to left, which stand above the name on almost every Jewish tombstone and are the abbreviation for *Poh niqbar*, "Here is buried." When the artist resumes his work of inscription, now reluctantly and imperfectly because of the resistance of his subject, the first visible consequence is a single capital letter, *J*. As it happens, this is the one letter of the Latin alphabet that has a German name almost the phonetic equivalent of the corresponding Hebrew letter—German *Jot* and Hebrew *yod*. But we are scarcely given the chance to construe this *J* as the first letter of the ineffable name of God (Kafka would surely have been familiar with the designation *J* for Yahwist, made famous by German biblical scholarship), for "at long last K. understood him." What he understands, of course, is that the *J* is the initial letter of his own given name, and the moment K. submits to his fate of interment, everything changes radically:

earth turns into water, *einer sanften Strömung*, a gentle current that buoys him up—one recalls the coffin-beds in Benjamin—as he plunges into his own grave, and the remaining letters of this name now race over the stone in grand flourishes.

Unlike the Benjamin dream, there is no prominent erotic motif here, unless, in Freudian zeal, an interpreter chooses to make one out of the plunge into the hole and the experience of being gently wafted at the end. In Benjamin's dream thanatos is in the background, eros in the foreground; in K.'s dream it is the other way around. A link between the two texts is the peculiar sense of euphoria associated with the inscription of letters in a landscape of sarcophagi: both the real Walter Benjamin and the fictional Joseph K. awake from their dreams enchanted. In the Benjamin dream, as we saw, the father is present through the token of the panama hat. In the dream Kafka invents for his character, there is no evident trace of Hermann Kafka or a fictional equivalent. The artist in the scene cannot have the force of a father figure because in Kafka's experience and in his imaginative world the paternal and the artistic are emphatically opposed realms. But the system of seemingly arbitrary, unbending authority in which Joseph K. of *The Trial* is entrapped is surely the projection of the father-principle into a whole hydra-headed legal and social apparatus. The distraught mortuary artist, like the two nameless men who carry in the tombstone, is one of the many petty executives of that system. *Hier ruht* belongs to the language of the father, just as the name that is inscribed below it, beginning with the shaky *J* on the left and moving to the right, is the name that has been bestowed on him by the father. A death sentence is spelled out by those letters, but Joseph K., like Georg Bendemann in "The Judgment," experiences a release from the anguish of resistance in submitting to the sentence: as the first small stroke of the *J* is inscribed, he feels a sense of relief, *eine Erlösung*, which in other contexts can also mean "deliverance," "redemption."

This was not the first time Kafka had pondered tombstones and mortuary inscriptions as an image of his own blocked fate. Several years before the composition of "A Dream," in his diary entry for December 15, 1910, he noted the following about his emotional condition and his vocation as a writer. "It is as if I were made of stone, as if I were my own tombstone, there is no loophole for doubt or for faith, for love or repugnance, for courage or anxiety, in particular or in general, only a vague hope lives on, but no better than the inscriptions on tombstones."[19] What the fictional dream does is to transform the tombstone from dead end into inviting exit, to a large degree through the striking prominence it gives to the act of alphabetic inscription.

I am not proposing that either "A Dream" or *The Trial* is explicitly concerned with Jewish identity or with the opposition between German and Hebrew. Joseph K. is driven to the point where death becomes the one way out by other vectors—by his moral character, his propensity to evasion of responsibility; by his manipulative, instrumental relation to other human beings and the state of fundamental isolation in which it puts him; by the gnawing insecurity of his self-destructive psychology. All this makes perfectly coherent reading without reference to Kafka's Jewish background. My aim here, however, is not to propose an "intrinsic" interpretation of the text but to try to see it as a document that reflects the writer's cultural predicament. The "deliverance" of Joseph K.'s dream-death is determined by a variety of causes inferable from the novel, but the particular agency of the dream-death is script read from left to right: the displacement of *peh nun* by *Hier ruht* is an emblem of the self-alienation that makes existence unlivable for the Kafka protagonist, both here and elsewhere in his fiction.

All three writers manifest a certain apprehension of strangeness regarding their mother tongue: it is near and dear to each as his most subtle instrument of expression, and yet it sometimes seems a discomfiting or even menacing language of otherness. Perhaps the most extreme and extravagant statement of this linguistic malaise is Kafka's assertion in a diary entry (October 24, 1911, shortly after his discovery of the Yiddish theater) that his Jewish mother could not really be a *Mutter*, and that the necessity of calling her that introduced a small wedge of psychological distance, prevented him from loving her as fully as he might have. Benjamin in all likelihood felt this linguistic ambivalence far less acutely, but it was sufficiently present in his consciousness that he was drawn from German to French as subject, going as far as the crossover of languages in the dream-letter; and, beyond such European transactions, he meditated on the idea of a primal cosmic language that was the abiding matrix for all merely national and historical divisions of speech. In Scholem, the potential alienation from German is realized in clear-cut biographical terms: on the verge of manhood he crosses over into Hebrew and soon thereafter emigrates to Palestine; when he comes back on a visit to Germany in 1946 after more than twenty years, he discovers that in this time span, half of it under a totalitarian regime, his native language has changed into something ugly and unfamiliar.[20]

I suspect that the uneasiness about German, coupled with an imposing brilliance in using it, is an important element in the modernism of each of these writers. For literary modernism in general oscillates—sometimes even in the work of a single writer—between a radical skepticism about the efficacy of language, a virtual alienation from language, and an intoxication with language, a reveling in its expressive, mimetic, and aesthetic possibilities. Joyce, Proust, Hermann Broch are among the inebriants of language, perhaps sometimes to their detriment; Beckett, the disciple of Joyce and Proust, drives the impulse of unsparing skepticism as far as it can go. But even the celebratory modernists cannot take the adequacy of language for granted: it must be pulled out of its conventional shapes on the level of diction, syntax, imagery, and, in the extreme instance of *Finnegans Wake*, even on the level of morphemes, phonemes, and constituent words, in order to convey the authority of the writer's vision of the world. The peculiar cultural location of the Jewish writer in German, enamored of his language and literary tradition, in one respect deeply rooted in them, and yet also troubled by a sense of actual or potential difference, makes him a modernist writ large. On the formal and thematic level, this sense of divided identity, particularly in respect to language, is reflected in the oneiric, the parabolic, and the narratively and stylistically iconoclastic elements of Kafka's fiction; in Scholem's sustained argument for the centrality of the aberrant in Jewish history and in his manifold investigations of all that he subsumed under the rubric of "abyss"; in Benjamin's gnomically expressed vision of the breakdown of tradition and the decay of experience, in his pursuit of the "detritus of history" as the key to its hidden nature.

If living and writing in the terrific tensions of the paradoxes of language are characteristic modernist acts, the peculiar focus on the forms of the written word may well be a distinctively Jewish emphasis. Jewish tradition perpetuated itself above all by a concentration on and an exfoliation from the written word. Literary and archaeological evidence suggests that writing goes back to an early and determinative phase of the biblical period itself. The Talmud, though designated the "oral Torah," is passed on and studied as a written text, eventually accorded a special typographic format in which the text is elaborately surrounded with subtextual and marginal commentaries and supracommentaries. Visually, the tradition has only a minimal iconography but an abundant calligraphy and, after Gutenberg, an inventive typography as well. All three of our writers were keenly aware of the salience of the scriptorial in Jewish tradition, and that awareness was no doubt heightened by their having been reared in an antithetical system of inscription, from west to east. All shared the assumption that the written word was the clue to identity, and perhaps to a larger framework of meaning beyond identity. Scholem, attracted as a young student to the kabbalistic theory of language, pored over mystical texts in which combinations and permutations of Hebrew letters led the way to God, whether as elements of a theosophic system of knowledge or as trance-inducing devices for the ecstatic, and among the kabbalistic texts he edited in his early years was a mystical alphabet. Kafka and Benjamin were drawn in their own different ways to alphabetic epiphanies, but the Latin letters of their dream-visions—an incomplete *J*, the top of a *d*—provide ambiguous revelations, though the dreaming Benjamin overcomes the ambiguity by following out a fantasy of letter turned to matter, spirit into flesh. In any case, for all three writers, letters make words, words constitute texts, and the text is conceived as the primary object of knowledge—when you stop to think of it, by no means an inevitable assumption. Novelist, critic, historian, each casts himself, rather surprisingly, in the role of exegete. But the compelling power of the text and the consequent centrality of exegesis in these three literary enterprises are a topic that demands attention in its own right.

THREE

THE POWER OF
THE TEXT

Nothing quite compares with the attraction of working out an incisive interpretation of a text.

Gershom Scholem to Walter Benjamin,
September 19, 1933

One of the odd little meditations in Benjamin's *One-Way Street* lays bare the peculiar relation to textuality that he shared with Kafka and Scholem—all three of them being like Klee's *Angelus Novus* in Benjamin's reading of the painting, modernists with their faces turned toward the backward vista of tradition, while the winds of history inexorably blow them forward away from the Eden of origins. The meditation appears under the uppercase rubric CHINESE CURIOS, though the Chinese connection is not made until the last sentence. Benjamin begins, instructively, with an analogy for two modes of taking in a text, drawn from a contrast between the pretechnological and the technological. "The power of a country road is different when one is walking along it from when one is flying over it by airplane. In the same way, the power of a text is different when it is read from when it is copied out." Benjamin goes on in the next two sentences to spell out how only the pedestrian is able to experience from moment to moment the fine gradations of variety of the changing landscape, and then he concludes by applying his comparison to copyist over against reader:

Only the copied text thus commands the soul of him who is occupied with it, whereas the mere reader never discovers the new aspects of his inner self that are opened by the text, that road cut through the interior jungle forever closing behind it: because the reader follows the movement of his mind in the free flight of daydreaming, whereas the copier submits it to command. The Chinese practice of copying books was thus an incomparable guarantee of literary culture, and the transcript a key to China's enigmas.[1]

Reading without copying has of course always been a common option attractive for its speed and convenience, but the nearly universal separation between the two is the consequence of a technological innovation, the invention of printing. Thus an instance of twentieth-century technology, man traveling speedily and conveniently by air over a landscape he now barely experiences, is an appropriate figure for the postscribal reader. China as the emblem of premodern culture, perhaps the vehicle of a vital transmissible wisdom, is an image Benjamin shares with Kafka. For both, China is a displacement toward the universal of Judaism, the scribal culture closer to hand that both sought intermittently to appropriate: the exotic writing on parchment from right to left is displaced into a still more exotic code of inscription from top to bottom. Benjamin's key assumption in this reflection should be underscored: the text has the power to reveal to the reader "new aspects of his inner self," but only if he assimilates it in the most studied slow motion, stroke by elegant stroke, through a process frankly described as submission to its authority. There is something tangled, blocked in the reader that the inscribed text can open up. Kafka in one of his letters describes this opening up in the more violent image of an ax cutting through the ice to the frozen inner zone of the reader, and he invents a kind of satanic parody of that process in the infernal machine of "In the Penal Colony" that inscribes the condemned man's sentence in his body with a horrific array of needles.

If the painstaking labor of the scribe is the perfect model of fealty to the text, all three writers were acutely aware of another mode of intimate dwelling with the text characteristic of traditional culture that was much closer to their own enterprise as writers. That other mode is interpretation. Indeed, what repeatedly drew both Benjamin and Scholem to Kafka was his genius for setting the traditional categories of interpretation and interpretability at issue from an unblinking modernist perspective. It is precisely this fundamental aspect of Kafka that has proved most resistant to imitation. Many writers have sought to emulate his use of parable and fantasy; but without his uncanny insight into what is at stake in interpretation, such "Kafkaesque" fiction generally seems contrived and uncompelling.

Scholem himself emphatically placed Kafka in this light in his 1974 address to the Bavarian Academy of the Arts. In the years since his early emigration from Germany, he explained to his German audience, there were only three "books" that he had truly read—which is to say, reading in the manner of Benjamin's copyist, or reading as an interpreter—"over and over, with an open heart and in spiritual tension." These three bodies of texts were the Hebrew Bible; the Zohar, written in Aramaic; and one set of works in German, the collected writings of Franz Kafka. Scholem observes that this last group of texts exhibits a profound if peculiar affinity with the first two, which he characterizes as follows: "In substantial portions of his writing there is a kind of canonicity, that is to say, they are open to infinite interpretation; and many of them, especially the most impressive of them, constitute in themselves acts of interpretation."[2] The historical distribution and the differing character of these three instances of Jewish canon chosen by Scholem are probably not accidental. The Bible of course is the set of texts that stands at the moment of spiritual origins; it is the ultimate, overflowing source, the writings intensely interpreted by all subsequent generations as authoritative revelation. The Zohar, of all the major texts of postbiblical tradition, is the one that pushes interpretation to its most daring extremes, that constitutes the most radical possibility of reinterpretation in the midst of devout confirmation of the authority of the first revelation. Kafka, the exemplary Jewish modernist, raises fundamental questions about the validity of interpretation, conjures with the vertiginous possibility that we may be at the end of the line of interpretation, revelation now forever receding from us. Scholem needed all three of these instances of canonicity to define the limits of his own spiritual world.[3] The power to compel interpretation, put forth by Scholem as the chief criterion of canonicity, is, as we shall see, one of the governing assumptions of his thinking about tradition. It is important, however, first to understand clearly that the category of the canonical is not something merely imposed on Kafka by Scholem as exegete-reader but rather a notion that Kafka himself held quite consciously in mind, to which he aspired in his writing.

Kafka's observations in his diary on "The Judgment," a story he regarded as a breakthrough in his writing, are often cited by commentators as a guide to its interpretation. What I would like to stress here is not the content of the observations but the mode of interpretive reflection they represent. In his diary entry for February 11, 1913, triggered by reading the proofs of "The Judgment," which had been composed almost five months earlier in one feverish sitting on Yom Kippur night, Kafka records his sense of how "the story came out of me like a real birth, covered with filth and slime." The metaphor of birth, though it also has other strong implications, has the effect of severing the production of the story from the writer's volition. After its emergence from him as the consequence of an uncontrollable natural process, he is free to scrutinize it as an object, and at this point the birth-metaphor is dropped and the object in question is interrogated as something canonical rather than physical. Here is a characteristic sample from the entry:

> Georg has the same number of letters as Franz. In Bendemann, "mann" is a strengthening of "Bende" to provide for all the as yet unforeseen possibilities in the story. But Bende has exactly the same number of letters as Kafka, and the vowel *e* occurs in the same places as does the vowel *a* in Kafka.

Frieda has as many letters as F. [Felice] and the same initial, Brandenfeld has the same initial as B. [Bauer], and in the word "Feld" a certain connection of meaning, as well [i.e., *Bauer* means "farmer," *Feld* means "field"].[4]

This seems to me less interesting as autopsychoanalysis than as the perception of a certain mode of textuality. Every minute detail of the text, every vocable, is the marker of submerged meanings that the interpreter—even when he is the one from whom the text "came out"—can only begin to guess. The literal constitution of the text has a multifaceted authority: phonetic resemblances, the number and position of letters, semantic associations of words, all have their significance. Kafka is only a step away here from traditional Hebrew modes of exegesis such as *notarikon* (interpreting words as acrostics for sentences) and *gematria* (linking words with other words by reference to the numerical value of the constituent letters).

Toward the end of his life, in a diary entry dated January 16, 1922, Kafka makes his most daring admission that he has aspired to create a new sacred scripture—the fitting subject of exegesis—in his writing. His formulation is obscure, perhaps because he felt he was touching on an ultimate secret he could scarcely divulge even in the privacy of his notebooks. After speaking of the terrible isolation imposed by his writing, his sense of its having driven him to the verge of madness, he changes the image he has used for writing from "pursuit" to "assault," which he imagines "launched from below, from mankind" and also perhaps "from above, aimed at me from above." (This latter alternative is another way of separating the act of writing from volition, here intimating that writing may somehow be revelation "from above.") Kafka concludes his reflection in the following terms: "All such writing is an assault on frontiers; if Zionism had not intervened, it might easily have developed into a new secret doctrine, a Kabbalah. There are intimations of this. Though of course it would require genius of an unimaginable kind to strike root again in the old centuries anew and not spend itself withal, but only then begin to flower forth."

The remark about the intervention of Zionism is especially puzzling. I should think its most likely meaning is that the mere possibility of realizing his vocation as a Jew in the realm of the political here and now had somehow deflected Kafka from the unswerving dedication to the less possible task of building a bridge of words, as his ancestors had, to the unknowable realm of the transcendent: the concentration on the absolute had to be total, and even a momentary glance at the relative sphere of politics could throw it out of focus.

What is peculiar and, I would say, peculiarly Jewish in all this is Kafka's textualization of the truth. The Greeks, though they of course had their own elaborate textual traditions, ordered things differently, creating the conceptual tools for the empirical investigation of reality that would become the great enterprise of pure science and also, in the course of time, the matrix of Western technology. The distinctive strength as well as the drastic limitation of the Hebrew orientation, with a belief in revelation as its point of departure, was its commitment to deriving everything from the text rather than from the circumambient world: "Turn it over, and turn it over again, for everything is in it," according to Ben Bag-Bag's famous formulation in the Mishnah Avot. It is a principle whose workings Scholem studied for a lifetime, that often mesmerized Benjamin, and that Kafka absorbed into his very marrow.

Among the most revelatory expressions of Kafka's textualization of the truth are his paradoxical reflections on Scripture—the one point in his writing where he becomes exegete, or in some instances midrashist, in the most easily recognizable sense of the term. Although these very brief prose pieces are hardly in themselves a major aspect of Kafka's achievement, they provide a certain key to the peculiar operation of his fictional world. Let us consider his quirky meditation on the figure of Abraham, a moment in Kafka's writing that Benjamin noted with admiration. Kafka tries to imagine the Abraham of Genesis 22, enacting the scandal of faith as he responds to the outrageous call from God by preparing to sacrifice his beloved only son. Kierkegaard's intensely Christian reading of this story is obviously in the background. Against the awesome violation of the human quotidian reflected in the biblical tale, Kafka, marooned in ordinary existence and mentally straining after an impossibly removed realm of transcendence, conjures up a series of counter-Abrahams. "I could conceive of another Abraham for myself," he writes, "—he certainly would have never gotten to be a patriarch or even an old-clothes dealer—who was prepared to satisfy the demand for a sacrifice immediately, with the promptness of a waiter, but was unable to bring it off because he could not get away, being indispensable." Then he imagines other Abrahams, including some who "did not even have a son, yet already had to sacrifice him." At the heart of biblical awe Kafka discovers the grotesque: "These are impossibilities, and Sarah was right to laugh." From here, touching on other hypothetical Abrahams preoccupied with the building of their houses and averting their eyes from the distant mountain, Kafka proceeds to his profoundest, and most Kafkan, version of Abraham:

> But take another Abraham. One who wanted to perform the sacrifice altogether in the right way and had a correct sense in general of the whole affair, but could not believe that he was the one meant, he, an ugly old man, and the dirty youngster that was his child. True faith is not lacking to him, he has this faith; he would make the sacrifice in the right spirit if only he could believe he was the one meant. He is afraid that after starting out as Abraham with his son he would change on the way into Don Quixote. The world would have been enraged at Abraham could it have beheld him at the time, but this one is afraid that the world would laugh itself to death at the sight of him.[5]

Kafka's treatment of biblical texts sometimes clearly sub-
verts them, as, for example, his different versions of Babel,
including one called "The Pit of Babel" in which people dig a
pit, or mine (*Schlacht*) instead of building a tower, in a farce of
inverted aspiration ("Some progress must be made."). It is,
however, imprecise to say, as many critics have, using the
literary jargon of the hour, that Kafka "deconstructs" the biblical text. On the contrary, Kafka's imagination is compelled by
the structure of the biblical text and he walks around it, trying
to find some odd back-entrance into it for himself. Or, to shift
to Benjamin's metaphor, he tries to find ways in which it can
become a path into his interior jungle. There is nothing obviously funny about Genesis 22, but Kafka is quite right that
laughter flickers in the background of the surrounding stories
("Sarah was right to laugh."). First Sarah laughed in disbelief at
the promise of a child. Then, after giving birth to Isaac ("he-
who-laughs") in Genesis 21, she proclaims: "God has made
laughter for me; whoever hears will laugh with me [or "for me,"
or "at me"—the Hebrew preposition is an abyss of ambigu-
ity]." Although God grants the joy of maternity to a ninety-
year-old woman, the word-choices of the story suggest that
the divine gift may also entail reduction to a state of absurdity,
becoming an object of mockery in the startled eyes of the
world. Kafka's audacious insight as exegete is to see that the
absurd-making consequences of divine attention might be
transferred to the Binding of Isaac itself. The object of the
sacrifice here, *der schumtzige Junge*, the dirty youngster, sounds
vaguely like a figure in a Yiddish joke. This Abraham, unlike
the ones of Kafka's previous versions, who are enmired in
worldliness, has faith but not the self-confidence to believe he
is the one addressed by God, and he is afraid that the attempt
to live out the scandal of faith will turn him into a laugh-
ingstock. Kafka brilliantly defines this fear as Abraham's apprehension that he will turn into Don Quixote—the haunting
archetype created by modern skepticism, the man of passion-

ate, idealistic faith who fixes his gaze on mere chimeras, dooming himself to a destiny of futility and farce.

Benjamin's proposal that the comic aspects of Jewish theology might provide a key to Kafka is beautifully apposite here. Kafka's intention is not to stand the text on its head, as he does in "The Pit of Babel," but, as I have said, to find a way into the text, which addresses him with ineluctable if baffling authority. The procedure he adopts to this end is preeminently midrashic. Its outward sign is the contemporaneity and the concreteness of the narrative idiom—the Abraham who can't even manage to be an old-clothes dealer, the ugly old man with the dirty youngster, and, in the midrashic *mashal*, or parable, that follows the quoted passage, the worst student in the class who rises from his dirty desk in the last row to accept the award he mistakenly thinks was announced for him. The inward force of this whole midrashic procedure is to uncover hidden facets of the biblical text, creating a meaningful link between its distant, in some ways alien world and the world of its modern reader. In the biblical account, Abraham's confidence in his vocation of obedience to the Lord of heaven and earth is never in question, and his spiritual dignity is never in doubt, unless one wants to make exception for the two sister-bride episodes in which he figures as a somewhat awkward prevaricator. But the laughing, laughed-at character of old Sarah at his side suggests that certain indignities may attend those whose lives become entangled with God's inscrutable aims. It is those indignities that Kafka, the half-believer or would-be believer who could never believe in himself, seizes on as his own point of entry into the spiritual dilemmas expressed in the text.

If one were to formulate his perception as a theological principle, it would sound something like this: the irruption of the transcendent into the paltry realm of the human—"the assault from above"—always produces radical discrepancies, of which the human subject becomes acutely aware as he is conscious of his paltriness. Thus the encounter between Creator and creature repeatedly exhibits a comic potential, which may range from the comedy of grace improbably vouchsafed (old Sarah laughing, happy in her absurdity) to cruel farce (Joseph the foreordained elect fleeing naked from the lustful grasp of Potiphar's wife—a scene Kafka carefully imitated in *Amerika*).

The peculiar genius of Kafka's novels is to fuse narrative invention with exegesis, making the fiction a constant contemplation of its own perplexing meanings, with the perplexed protagonist repeatedly seen in the absurdity of his efforts of contemplation. Kafka elevates exegesis to a universal and exclusive mode of cognition and at the same time parodies it, raising doubts as to whether it has any ground in a revealed truth. The famous first sentence of *The Trial* is the statement of a supposition: "Someone must have traduced Joseph K., for without having done anything wrong he was arrested one fine morning." The critic Stanley Corngold sets this in exactly the right perspective by observing that "the narrative begins not with the first event of the plot but with a first interpretation of the event."[6] In all three of Kafka's novels, event is ancillary to interpretation: this is why these books are so disquieting; this is also why they are often vaguely funny, even as they become menacing.

The last of the three novels, *The Castle*, is the most striking instance of a world suffused with, and perhaps also corroded by, exegesis. In the opening pages, K. has scarcely arrived at the inn when he overhears a certain young man named Schwarzer, in a phone conversation with the Castle, referring to him as the Land-Surveyor—the very identity he has been trying to establish. The use of this single term sends him into an exegetical whirl:

K. pricked up his ears. So the Castle had recognized him as the Land-Surveyor. That was unpropitious for him, on the one hand, for it meant that the Castle was well informed about him, had estimated all the probable chances, and was taking up the challenge with a smile. On the other hand, however, it was quite propitious, for if his interpretation was right they had underestimated his strength, and he would have more freedom of action than he dared hope. And if they expected to cow him by their lofty superiority in recognizing him as Land-Surveyor, they were mistaken; it made his skin prickle a little, that was all.[7]

Recent criticism has properly stressed the importance in Kafka's fictional world of the narrative technique of *erlebte Rede*, or narrated monologue. Its utility in evoking an exegetical reality is paramount. Intertwining as it does the grammatical and temporal perspective of a third-person narrator with the inward utterance of the protagonist, it gives us the bare semblance of an authoritative viewpoint continuously undermined by the doubting subjectivity of the character. K., picking up his single verbal clue, leaps to an inference that is by no means certain ("So the Castle had recognized him"), then goes on in characteristic fashion to weigh contradictory alternatives ("on the one hand," "on the other hand"). The scrutiny of suppositions of this virtually talmudic procedure—by this late point in his life Kafka had actually made a preliminary acquaintance with the Talmud—is emphasized by the prominence of if-clauses and by the explicit statement, "if his interpretation was right." I have chosen this passage as an illustration because it makes the operation of an exegetical process particularly clear, but that process continues relentlessly throughout *The Castle*; there are hundreds of analogues to this early moment. Quite often, as here, K. is interrogating an actual verbal text—a scrap of telephone conversation overheard, a written note, a rumor. Elsewhere the object of anxious and perhaps quite wild interpretation is an act, a gesture, or a piece of imperfect visual information—an image glimpsed through a peephole, the view or mirage of the Castle itself looming above in the distance through wavering veils of fog and snow and darkness.

All this exegetical activity constantly spills over from the narrated monologue into the dialogue. Indeed, if *The Castle*, as Marthe Robert has ingeniously argued, is a kind of archetypal recapitulation of the tradition of the European novel,[8] the most striking way in which it departs from that tradition is in its radical transformation of the use of dialogue. In the realist novel, dialogue is above all the kinetic revelation of individuality and the representation of how distinctive individual presences impinge on each other, respond to each other, affect each other in the defining context of a shared social and cultural system. In Kafka there is no shared system, and his central characters are isolates, not individuals. The interaction of individual personalities of realist dialogue is displaced by a collision of exegetical viewpoints. His characters, especially in *The Castle*, repeatedly argue or trade hypotheses about what things, or actual texts, mean. This is a world of elaborately argued conjecture constantly shadowed by the suspicion that the conjectures are wrong. "You misconstrue everything," the landlady at one point tells K., "even a person's silence" (p. 105). Formally, the dialogues are often cast not as rapid interchange but as long disquisitions in which each of the interlocutors spins out an argument for several pages.

Thus K., after hearing one such disquisition from Olga expressing her suppositions about Barnabas' relations with the Castle, proclaims his agreement with her line of interpretation before he goes on to elaborate one of his own: "Here I think you've touched on the essential point . . . After all you've told me, I believe I can see the matter clearly. Barnabas is too young for this task. Nothing he tells you is to be taken seriously at its face value" (pp. 238–239). As this last remark suggests, exegesis acts as a solvent in Kafka's world, steadily eating away the foundation of knowledge even as it seems to promise access to knowledge ("I think you've touched on the essential point"). The exemplary moment, in which exegesis is seen to reach its zero-degree, occurs in an exchange between K. and the

Mayor. The Mayor has been expounding his theory of the limited meaning of a letter from the Castle official Klamm because the message in question is "only a private letter" and not an official communication. K., an exegete with a different agenda, is exasperated by this line of reasoning: "Mr. Mayor . . . you interpret the letter so well that nothing remains of it but a signature on a blank sheet of paper" (p. 92).

No novelist has had so shrewd an insight as Kafka into the absurdity, the risibility, and the desperate urgency of man as *homo significans*, the animal that makes meanings. His awareness of the salience of textuality in Jewish culture surely contributed a great deal to this central insight. His fiction hovers between two comic possibilities, one theological and the other nihilistic. If the text under scrutiny is in fact divine in origin, there is a scandalous chasm between Addresser and addressee, and the act of reception is necessarily an absurdity, though perhaps a fruitful absurdity, one that may provide vital spiritual sustenance. If the text is a mere thoughtless scrap of words tossed off by a capricious creature on the same uncertain footing of worldly transience as the interpreter, all the engines of interpretation will discover no more than an infinite regress of pointless enigmas, or the *reductio ad absurdum* of the blank page. These two possibilities correspond to what Benjamin saw as the two products of the "decay of wisdom" in Kafka, and I think Benjamin was right to assume that Kafka was not very sanguine about the first possibility—which Benjamin describes as "a sort of theological whispered intelligence dealing with matters discredited and obsolete."[9] The second possibility, in Benjamin's formulation, leads to "folly," a state devoid of the inner substance of wisdom but perpetuating its confident gestures, giving us back, I would say, Abraham as Don Quixote, Moses as Charlie Chaplin.

If Kafka founds a whole fictional world on the spiritual problematic of interpretation, exposing both its necessity and its potential absurdity, Benjamin exhibits a kind of knowing nostalgia for the ideal of interpretation. "Commentary and translation," he remarks in *One-Way Street*, "stand in the same relation to the text as style and mimesis to nature: the same phenomenon considered from different aspects. On the tree of the sacred text both are only the eternally rustling leaves; on that of the profane, the seasonally falling fruits."[10] Here again, Benjamin's choice of simile is instructive about his way of conceiving things. He is prepared to imagine a nice correspondence between text and nature—which may be thought of, as I proposed earlier, as the typical objects of attention respectively of the Hebraic and the Hellenic mind. (If we place those two terms in relation to the two writers who mattered most to Benjamin, Kafka represents the most comprehensive working-out in fiction of the attachment to text through commentary, and Proust, as supreme stylist and master of mimesis, brilliantly encompasses "nature"—moral behavior, humanity in the integument of social institutions, the subtle flow of consciousness, and also the natural world.) At least here, Benjamin can confidently envision a possibility of organic connection between the commenting or translated word and the original text: for the sacred text, timeless in relevance, commentary is the evergreen foliage, a living extension of the eternal tree (itself a kabbalistic image); but even for the profane text, commentary bears fruit. The image of tree and leaves also stresses the secondary status of commentary, but it is a healthy, productive secondariness.

The odd thing about Benjamin's relation to exegesis is that he speculated about it, contemplated it as an ideal of writing and cognition, without ever quite getting around to practicing it. His remarkable essays on Kafka, Proust, Baudelaire, Karl Kraus, and his longer study of the Baroque *Trauerspiel* involve abundant quotation, but for the most part to illustrate metaphysical speculations or historical generalizations rather than to set texts for exposition through commentary. Abstaining from actual exegesis, he mused on the linguistic matrix that could give it ultimate grounding. He was enchanted by the idea that the words of all texts, sacred and profane, could lead back to a cosmic language of origin, and this notion was by no means limited to the intensely metaphysical ruminations of his early years. Thus, in his 1931 essay on Karl Kraus, squarely in the middle of his Marxist phase, he proposes the odd but arresting idea that only in the interpenetration of discourses involved in quotation is language consummated: "In it is mirrored the angelic tongue in which all words, startled from the idyllic context of meaning, have become mottoes in the book of Creation."[11]

The "book of Creation" is of course an old Christian cliché in most of the European languages, but it is also, as Benjamin would surely have known through Scholem, the precise translation for the title of a classic kabbalistic text, *Sefer Yetsirah*. A scrutiny of his writing, including the letters and the autobiographical pieces, raises the suspicion that he never enacted the vocation of commentator because it was associated in his mind with a kind of private messianic prospect. Scholem himself comes close to making such a judgment when he observes that the commentary on "Hebrew texts of the Jewish tradition" represented for Benjamin "a sort of utopian vanishing point."[12] That is, he saw true commentary as a concentration on sacred rather than profane texts, its proper exemplar the Kabbalist or the medieval Hebrew exegete. This is why in his meeting with Judah Magnes and Scholem in Paris in 1927 he could wax enthusiastic over the notion of mastering Hebrew and fully realizing his gifts by commenting on Hebrew texts, though, for reasons we have already seen, this was an alluring prospect with which he beguiled his flagging spirits, not a goal he was ever deeply prepared inwardly to achieve.

For Benjamin the cultural and spiritual task of commentary was profoundly implicated in the urgent question of our human capacity to apprehend the past, to establish a living connection with it. This was indeed the central question that exercised both him and Scholem throughout their careers. It was also an implicit concern of Kafka's, whose fiction could be construed as a definitive representation of the breakdown of confident tradition, but in his novels and stories Kafka removed the problem of exegesis from the context of history, offering atemporal images of man trapped in a labyrinth of ambiguous messages he is compelled to decipher. For Benjamin, the confrontation between exegete and text, present and past, is gravely complicated by a tension between the perception of fragments from the standpoint of the present and a presupposition of integral wholeness on the part of the original makers and users of the traditional text. In his book on the German Baroque, he makes the fascinating suggestion— especially fascinating in light of what we have observed about the consciousness of alphabets and exotic script—that the sacred text achieves its ideal form in hieroglyphics, which is to say, in graphic complexes that are visually apprehended as integral wholes.[13] We, on the other hand, inhabit a cultural and historical reality in which all experience is reduced to bits and pieces, our mental horizon fixed by a system of alphabetic transcription that makes texts conglomerations of discrete letters. Our world of fragments, moreover, is not naturalized by consciousness but perceived as malaise, crisis, alienation, radical disorientation (this idea variously informs Benjamin's essays on Baudelaire, Proust, Kafka, and Surrealism). How, then, are we to take in the past, to comment on the wholeness of its sacred texts? In the "Epistemo-Critical Prologue" to his study of the *Trauerspiel*, Benjamin offers a haunting and pessimistic image of what it is that moderns are constrained to do with the past: "Just as a man lying sick with fever transforms all the words which he hears into the extravagant images of delirium, so it is that the spirit of the present age seizes on the manifestations of past or distant spiritual worlds, in order to take possession of them and unfeelingly incorporate them into its own self-absorbed fantasizing."[14]

In his last piece of writing, the "Theses on the Philosophy of History," composed in the spring of 1940 scant months before his suicide, Benjamin was still turning over this troubling idea, an idea that made mockery of the spiritually necessary act of exegesis. Now, however, he was groping toward a reconciliation between those "distant worlds" of the past and the compulsion of the present to appropriate mere fleeting fragments of the past for its own desperate needs. "The past can be seized," he observes in the fifth Thesis, "only as an image which flashes up at the instant when it can be recognized and is never seen again." The imaginative process that Benjamin had described in his essay on Baudelaire as a distinctively modern poetics of shock is here proposed as the *only* mode through which the past persists in the present. "For every image of the past that is not recognized by the present as one of its own concerns threatens to disappear irretrievably."[15] He goes on in his next Thesis to say—again intimating a metaphor of photographic or stroboscopic instantaneity—that the historical articulation of the past does not mean representing the past "the way it really was" but rather is the attempt "to seize hold of a memory as it flashes up at a moment of danger." In anticipation of certain critical currents in contemporary historiography, he suggests that what the historian must do is uncover in the past what is muted, suppressed, marginalized, which bears on the urgency of the present: "In every era the attempt must be made anew to wrest tradition away from a conformism that is about to overpower it." This programmatic assertion then leads to one of the most famous statements of the "Theses": "A historical materialist . . . regards it as his task to brush history against the grain."[16]

Although Benjamin offers this last striking image as a metaphor for the critical perspective of the Marxist historian, David Biale has quite aptly adopted it as the epigraph of his admirable book on Scholem, and, indeed, one could scarcely summarize more incisively what it is that Scholem did with

Jewish history. (It is also one of the chief justifications for calling him a "modernist" among historians, as I have been doing.) But before turning to Scholem's own articulation of text and commentary, past and present, I would like to propose that Benjamin's notion of seizing an image of the past as it flashes up in a moment of danger has implications not only for the historian but also for the transmitter of tradition. What is at issue is whether tradition is intrinsically stable, even inert, and hence inevitably constraining, or whether it might not itself be a dynamic process, a wrestling with the limitations of its own origins, a kinetic crystallization of changing moments of danger. The earlier Benjamin appears to have entertained a conservative idea of tradition as something fixed and perhaps inviolable, as his images of the tree and the hieroglyph may suggest. With tradition so conceived, commentary can be no more than a tantalizing mirage, for the modern on his sickbed will necessarily twist out of shape the words he grasps in the paroxysms of his own spiritual fever. It is no wonder that Benjamin was mesmerized by the ideal of exegesis but never undertook it as a vocation. At the end of his life, however, he evidently began to think that this state of fever was not just a symptom of modernity but the condition of humanity at all times, immersed in the dangerous medium of history. Such a perception would certainly have jibed with the findings of his friend Gerhard about Jewry in the Mediterranean world of late antiquity, or in the Rhineland, France, Provence, and Iberia in the Middle Ages. If tradition, including the tradition deemed canonical in the proper theological sense of the term, is actually a dynamic response to history, daring and at times revolutionary in the treatment of its antecedents, commentary is no longer a delusion but a constantly available vehicle for innovation in a cultural system of overarching continuity.

This, in the drastic simplification of summary, is the general conclusion Scholem came to about exegesis through a lifetime devoted to a body of mystical texts that are often set out in the form of commentary and supracommentary and only occasionally and imperfectly as systematic exposition. Moreover, he saw a meaningful if sometimes problematic correspondence between the traditional activity of commentary and his own scholarly enterprise as historian-exegete. Thus, in the letter he wrote to the publisher and patron of culture Salman Schocken in 1937 on the occasion of Schocken's sixtieth birthday, he concedes the elusive nature of history itself and in the same breath affirms the indispensable value of commentary as the instrument for grasping historical truth: "Certainly, history may seem to be fundamentally an illusion, but an illusion without which in temporal reality no insight into the essence of things is possible. For today's man, that mystical totality of 'truth' (*des Systems*), whose existence disappears particularly when it is projected into historical time, can only become visible in the purest way in the legitimate discipline of commentary and in the singular mirror of philological criticism."[17]

The magisterial formulation of Scholem's conclusion about the role of commentary in Jewish tradition itself is his 1962 lecture at the Eranos Institute in Switzerland, "Revelation and Tradition as Religious Categories in Judaism." Of all Scholem's writings, I suspect it is the one that would have spoken most profoundly to Benjamin.

Scholem's global description of the peculiar orientation of Judaism toward truth begins on familiar ground, though with a vivifying power of acute definition. Since credally and conceptually everything in Jewish tradition originates at Sinai, in revelation, "everything that can come to be known has already been deposited in a timeless substratum." The depositing that Scholem has in mind, it should be stressed, is in the medium of words. "Truth," he goes on to say, "is given once and for all, and it is laid down with precision." Again, I would add that he means verbal precision. "Fundamentally, truth merely needs to be transmitted." From this perspective, the figure whom Scho-

lem calls "the seeker after truth" must submit himself to the
power of the text, just as Benjamin's copyist bows to the
"command" of the text. As a result, there is very little latitude
for the development of autonomous discourse not directly
subordinated to the authority of the revealed text: "Not system but *commentary* [Scholem's emphasis] is the legitimate form
through which truth is approached."[18]

This characterization suggests a posture of subservience on
the part of the transmitter or recipient or commentator toward
the originating text, and that is in fact the standard ideological
position, or conscious attitude, of rabbinic Judaism. The bold-
ness of Scholem's argument is to propose that commentary,
which presents itself as a mere supplement to the text, a dutiful
application or extension or illumination of it, is actually an
explosive force of change. In Scholem's lapidary formulation,
it is almost always the case for Judaism that "truth must be
brought forth from the text," but it is in the nature of texts that
this truth is never self-evident, must always be brought out by
a process of commentary, which means practically that there
are many truths in the text to be variously elicited according
to the historical standpoint, the method of analysis, the conceptual and spiritual assumptions of the interpreter. "What had
originally been believed to be consistent, unified, and self-
enclosed now becomes diversified, multifold, and full of contradictions."[19] This dynamic is a feature of all interpretation,
manifesting itself during the formative stage of postbiblical
Judaism in the legal and homiletic commentaries of the early
rabbis that would come to seem normative. Mystical interpretation merely pushes that dynamic to its logical extreme by
its insistence on the infinite interpretability of every word of
the Written Torah: "the word of God carries infinite meaning,
however it may be defined. Even that which has already
become a sign in the strict sense, and is already a mediated
word, retains the character of the absolute." As a result, the
metaphorical designation of tradition as oral Torah takes on

special significance in the kabbalistic view, putting as it does the fluidity of speech in place of the fixity of writing, "precisely because every stabilization in the text would hinder and destroy the infinitely moving, the constantly progressing and unfolding element within it, which would otherwise become petrified."[20]

Just as Benjamin's "Theses on the Philosophy of History" may make him sound like a latter-day historian of suppressed cultural voices, Scholem's account of text and interpretation, at least at first glance, makes him seem, a decade before the spread of the vogue, like a poststructuralist literary theorist. The text cannot be and should not be a stable entity. A gap always yawns between signifier and signified, however the interpreter seeks to close it; or, in another recension of contemporary theory, the meanings of the text are always established arbitrarily and conventionally by changing communities of interpretation. Kafka, too, anticipated this vista of skepticism about interpretation, but with a sense of dread and despair very different from the note of celebration often found in the recent literary theorists. In Scholem, however, there is another emphasis: initially, it stands in the background of his argument, but it emerges at the end as the conceptual axis on which everything else turns. The classical Jewish scholars, he observes near the beginning of his essay, perceived "revelation not as a unique and clearly delineated occurrence, but rather as a phenomenon of eternal fruitfulness to be unearthed and examined." Their achievement in the light of this perception was to establish "a tradition rooted in the Torah and growing out of it, a prime example of spontaneity in receptivity."[21] Much has been said by recent theorists of reading and writing about spontaneity, the often invoked "play of the signifiers," but the other key term in Scholem's statement is receptivity, which is the appropriate response to revelation. It would be foolish to assume any simple equation between Scholem's own perspective and the understanding of tradition of its pious

proponents, but at the very end of his essay the two viewpoints virtually merge. Scholem, who often made a point in
conversation of denying he was a secularist and even of expressing skepticism about the long-term viability of any thor-
oughgoing skepticism, remains a stubborn, heterodox the-
ist—as the earlier Benjamin was and as the later Benjamin
intermittently still played with being. He presupposes a divine
absolute that humanity seeks to encounter, that it must encounter in order to achieve a true sense of its place in the
scheme of things.

My guess is that Scholem would not have claimed revelatory exclusivity for the Jewish tradition, but he saw this tradition as a powerful articulation in language—"laid down with
precision"—of the human encounter with the divine. From
some of his comments on the Hebrew language, he may well
have perceived it as a uniquely effective vehicle for the conveying of such encounters. The great cosmogonic rhythms of
Genesis 1, followed by the story of the Garden in the next two
chapters, would not have been in his view mere chains of arbitrary signifiers or curiously wrought braids of ancient folklore,
myth, and etiological tales but eternally compelling statements, however antique the idiom, about the origin of the
world and humankind and the abiding perplexities of humanity's moral condition. Scholem stressed, both in "Revelation
and Tradition" and in *Origins of the Kabbalah*, the mystical idea
(he also called it magical and primitive) that the Torah was
made up of the infinite names of God, a divine language
without grammar. This is hardly an idea he could have literally
believed in himself, but, as he made clear in his 1926 letter to
Franz Rosenzweig, he did take quite seriously the notion that
the old Hebrew names for things were saturated with special
spiritual potencies: *shamayim*, heaven; *ruaḥ*, wind/spirit; *tehom*,
abyss; *'adamah*, earth; *tselem*, image; *da'at*, knowledge; and all
the rest of the haunting vocabulary of beginnings in Genesis.

The meanings of this complex of names had to be multi-faceted, and in the course of time, as later interpreters scrutinized the text from the perspective of their own sundry "moments of danger," the most astonishing new possibilities would be opened out from the words and the images of the original text. But Scholem's essential point, I think, is that this opening out was performed not as free play or as a willful imposition of alien ideas on the text but rather from a state of receptivity, a finely attuned attentiveness to ancient words that are deemed to have absolute authority. And Scholem does not discount the claim to authority. "In the Jewish conception," he says in the conclusion of his essay, "genuine tradition, like everything that is creative, is not the achievement of human productivity alone. It derives from a bedrock foundation." This statement describes the viewpoint of the tradition itself, but Scholem goes on to generalize about the abiding value of the tradition in terms that are guarded but ultimately theological, expressing his own understanding of how spiritual truth is to be sought in culture: "The tradition is one of the great achievements in which relationship of human life to its foundations is realized It is the living contact in which man takes hold of ancient truth and is bound to it, across all generations, in the dialogue of giving and taking."[22] Harold Bloom observes somewhere that tradition is the mask of continuity that cultural change assumes, but Scholem was persuaded that there was substance to the continuity, however startling the turns in the historical dialogue between present and past.

As one might infer from Bloom's relation to Scholem, or that of the neo-Marxists to Benjamin, or that of virtually every literary avant-garde movement since the 1940s to Kafka, latter-day intellectuals express a pronounced tendency to convert all three writers into prophets of our own postmodernist dilemmas. I hardly want to dismiss their contemporary relevance, but it is important to keep in mind that especially in regard to one crucial consideration the three men were deeply rooted in the spiritual concerns of the German-Jewish sphere of the early twentieth century. The modern Jewish awakening in Russia was by and large the awakening of a sense of people-hood—Zionism and Bundism, Hebraism and Yiddishism—whereas in Germany it characteristically took the form of a renewed interest in Judaism, a quest for God. Kafka, Benjamin, and Scholem were all in contact with Martin Buber and had some sympathy for his enterprise, though they voiced various and sometimes vehement reservations about the man and his thought. Both Benjamin and Scholem were keenly interested in the neotraditionalist theology of Franz Rosenzweig (Kafka did not live long enough to become acquainted with it), though Scholem objected to Rosenzweig's peculiarly ecclesiastical conception of Judaism. The postwar period in which Benjamin and Scholem began their careers was the time when a whole circle of young intellectuals had gathered around Rosenzweig's Freies Jüdisches Lehrhaus in Frankfurt; when the psychoanalyst Frieda Reichmann was running a sanatorium in Heidelberg that mingled the principles of Freud and Orthodox Judaism; when figures such as the psychological theorist Erich Fromm and the Frankfurt School sociologist Leo Lowenthal were flirting, however briefly, with Jewish faith. The theological world view that this whole milieu was seeking to articulate underlies the thinking of all three of our writers. In the case of Benjamin, it was so firmly anchored that not even the adherence to dialectic materialism could altogether dislodge it.[23] Kafka, who played the role of a perplexed guide to the perplexed for Scholem and Benjamin, was a more radical skeptic about theological truth than either of them—something of which they were perfectly aware. Or perhaps one should say that he represented the pole of uncompromising skepticism in their own oscillations about faith and tradition. As Scholem put it succinctly in the last of his "Ten Ahistorical Theses on the Kabbalah," Kafka created a kind of "heretical

Kabbalah," for he "gave expression to the borderline between religion and nihilism."[24]

The religion side of the line—and it is clearly not religion at large but Judaism, however universalized the fictional vehicle—is marked by Kafka's uncanny recreation of the conceptual categories and intellectual processes of religious tradition. Exegesis, I have argued, is the central case in point, and there is one Kafka parable on exegesis in which, with full openness to the possibilities of nihilism, he also makes contact with Scholem's view of tradition and commentary. The parable, "Prometheus," focuses on a story from Greek mythology, but the interpretive dynamic it exposes is the same that drives Kafka's meditations on Eden, Babel, Abraham, Sinai, and the Messiah. Four versions, *Sagen,* of Prometheus are proposed. The first is simply the plot of the traditional myth. In the second, Prometheus, maddened by the tearing beaks of the eagles, presses himself against the rock until he merges with it. The third and fourth versions are the radically skeptical ones: in the long course of time, eagles, hero, and gods are all forgotten; or, again, everyone grows weary of the whole eternal business, including the gods and the eagles and Prometheus' wound. But these two alternatives that drain all importance from the story are contrary to fact, for we continue to remember and to be deeply engaged by all these texts of origins. And so the parable concludes that even after Prometheus, gods, and eagles seem to evaporate, we are left with the inexplicable mass of rock, which the legend seeks to explain. "As it [the legend] came out of a substratum of truth it had in turn to end in the inexplicable."[25] Despite the dizzying perspectives opened up by his third and fourth versions of Prometheus, Kafka arrives at a *Wahrheitsgrund,* a "substratum of truth," not very different from the "bedrock foundation" Scholem sees as the matrix of tradition. As a Sinai displaced to the Caucasus, revelation removed to the borderline between religion and nihilism, it is not a ground of truth that can yield any reassuring answers, but precisely because it is inexplicable, it will eternally compel urgent questions. Perhaps, one may presume to infer from Scholem, that is what the original revelation, stripped of the more comfortable pieties of institutionalized religion, was always all about.

FOUR

REVELATION AND MEMORY

ⵍⵍⵍ

The strange, mysterious, perhaps dangerous, perhaps saving comfort that there is in writing: it is a leap out of murderers' row; it is a seeing of what is really taking place. This occurs by a higher type of observation, a higher, not a keener type, and the higher it is and the less within reach of the "row," the more independent it becomes, the more obedient to its own laws of motion, the more incalculable, the more joyful, the more ascendant in its course.

Franz Kafka, *Diaries,*
January 27, 1922

In the summer of 1934, Benjamin went on one of his extended visits to Bertolt Brecht's country retreat in Svendborg, Denmark. The conversations of the two writers, which Benjamin tersely recorded in his notebook, wandered over a broad range of topics, from the state of Communism in the Soviet Union to the condition of contemporary European literature, to the fiction of Kafka. In early July, Benjamin gave Brecht the manuscript of his essay on Kafka. For three weeks the playwright was unwilling to say anything on the subject. When he finally broke his silence, he expressed strong reservations about the episodic form of the essay as well as about Kafka himself, whose work he found to contain "a number of very useful things" half-buried in a forest of "obscurantism." Benjamin, opening his copy of Kafka's stories at random to a miniature piece called "The Next Village," proposed that they put their opposing critical approaches to the test by interpreting a specific text. Brecht was hesitant about making any comment on the spot, but toward the end of the month their discussions came back to "The Next Village" as part of what Benjamin describes as "a long and heated debate on my Kafka." It is recorded in the notebook entry for August 31st, which begins with the report of one of Brecht's most outrageous statements—that Benjamin's essay on Kafka "advanced Jewish fascism" because it multiplied the obscurity around Kafka instead of reducing him to clarity and formulating "practicable proposals [!] that can be derived from his stories."[1] Here first is the entire Kafka text about which they contended:

My grandfather used to say: "Life is astoundingly short. To me, looking back over it, life seems so foreshortened that I scarcely understand, for instance, how a young man can decide to ride over to the next village without being afraid that—not to mention accidents—even the span of a normal happy life may fall far short of the time needed for such a journey."[2]

Both Brecht and Benjamin propose rather surprising readings of this little parabolic puzzle. Brecht's reading is ingenious and intellectual, Benjamin's intuitive and free-associative. Brecht arrives at his conclusion by ignoring a basic aspect of the text's discursive structure that is paramount for Benjamin's reading—the fact that the parable is presented as the speech of an old man, the grandfather, embedded in the speech of a young man, his grandson.

Brecht declares it a counterpart to the story of Achilles and the tortoise. Someone who composes the ride from its smallest particles—leaving aside all incidents—will never reach the next village. Life itself is too short for such a ride. But the error lies in the "someone." For just as the ride is deceptive, so, too, is the rider. And just as the unity of life is now done away with, so, too, is brevity. No matter how brief it may be. This makes no difference because a different person from him who started arrives at the village.[3]

Brecht converts "The Next Village" into a logical conundrum. He does this by seizing on the one point of similarity between Kafka's parable and the paradox of Achilles and the tortoise—the fact that in each the trajectory of the journey is conceived to be uncompletable. He compounds, moreover, the ancient paradox about infinitely analyzable motion and infinitely unattainable destination with a second paradox about the discontinuity of the human subject: "For just as the ride is deceptive, so, too, is the rider." That is, there is no compelling philosophic reason to assume that the continuous "I" of the rider is more than an illusion of consciousness, for self, like the molecules of brain and body, constantly changes through time. No act, then, is really ever completed by the same person who initiated it. This interpretation is undeniably clever, and it jibes with Brecht's inclination to discover "practicable" elements in Kafka—if not practicable for political purposes, as he suggested in their earlier conversation, then at least practicable for philosophic reflection. To reduce the enigmatic in Kafka to a strictly logical paradox is a way of eliminating the element of obscurity. The main problem with such a reading is that Kafka is not really a philosophic writer (in contrast, for example, to his ingenious but much less imposing imitator, J. L. Borges). He is repeatedly concerned with man's experiential perplexities rather than with the puzzlements produced by the defining categories of ontology and epistemology In "The Next Village" there is not the slightest hint that the grandfather has submitted the journey to a logical analysis into successively smaller particles, as in the ancient paradox of Achilles and the tortoise, or that the continuity as subject of the young man who undertakes the journey is at issue.

Benjamin's counterinterpretation of the parable picks up an implication of the text ignored by Brecht, and oddly but instructively relates that to one of his own characteristic concerns:

> For my part, I give the following interpretation: the true measure of life is remembrance. Retrospectively, it traverses life with the speed of lightning. As quickly as one turns back a few pages, it has gone back from the next village to the point where the rider decided to set off. He whose life has turned into writing, like old people's, likes to read this writing only backward. Only so does he meet himself, and only so—in flight from the present—can his life be understood.[4]

Benjamin's profound intuition about Kafka, here and elsewhere, is that even the seeming abstractions are wound tightly around an armature of powerfully concrete experience. In

contrast to Proust, the other commanding figure in Benjamin's
modern literary pantheon, Kafka only very rarely represents
anyone in the actual process of remembering, but the implicit
dimension of remembrance—personal, cultural, and racial—
is central to his work. On the simplest level, "The Next
Village" suggests that the older we get, the more memory
looms, the more quickly time seems to go by, until the grandfather can scarcely imagine a sufficient amount of time—
"life seems so foreshortened"—for the completion of even
the shortest journey: only the delusions of youth enable the
young rider to think there could be time enough to reach the
goal. But Benjamin, noting the grandfather's linking of the
sense of foreshortened life with the act of "looking back over
it," stresses that the lightning-quick impulse of remembrance
orients us away from the destination, back to the point of
origin: it is only here that the true self is discovered. This
notion, I would argue, is the determinative one for Benjamin's
whole conceptual world, underlying his reading of Kafka and
Proust, his understanding of history and tradition, his ac-
counts of the storyteller and of the decline of aura, and sum-
marized with ideogrammatic clarity in his meditation on
Klee's *Angelus Novus*. What is peculiar is that he should associate this idea with writing, or more specifically, with life turning
into writing, something hardly intimated either as image or as
theme in Kafka's text.

Writing exerts such a peculiar force in Benjamin's imagination that it immediately turns from trope to truth in his
analysis of the Kafka piece. Scrutiny of the printed word is
introduced as a simile for the rapid backward movement of
memory ("as quickly as one turns back a few pages"), but it is
then transformed into a literal statement about the condition
of old people: their life becomes writing, which can be properly deciphered only by reading backward to the beginning.
This strange notion resonates with a number of ideas that
Benjamin pondered early and late: the primacy of language

over being; the power of the text as a path into the tangled interior self; an arcane embroidered script as the ultimate revelation of self (matched, as we observed, by Kafka's dream-vision of the mortuary inscription of identity and fate); and perhaps also the perception of Hebrew as the vehicle for the discovery of a hidden identity, read backward, from right to left, from the dilemmas of a European cultural adulthood back to an illuminating point of origin.

If Benjamin loads the slender structure of "The Next Village" with a heavier freight of meaning than it can plausibly bear, that is because past and future, which are clearly the thematic antitheses of the parable, stand in such high tension to each other in his thinking. His Marxism, building on his earlier reflections on the Jewish messianic idea, logically should have pointed him toward a future horizon of utopian fulfillment, but there is scant evidence in his writing that he ever imagined such a prospect of historical redemption in any concrete way. On the contrary, like Scholem and Kafka he was mesmerized by the past, not only as it dynamically evolved into the present (although this, too, was an urgent concern) but also as it led back on a sinuous path to archaic origins. The last piece of writing he did, the "Theses on the Philosophy of History," is a last desperate attempt, still far from any satisfying resolution, to reconcile some idea of futurity with the fixation on the past.

This whole turning back toward origins was the fundamental expression of the rebellion against the German bourgeois patrimony that we noted earlier in regard to all three writers. The controlling cultural concept of that legacy, as George Mosse has observed, is the idea of *Bildung*—moral-aesthetic education by gradual steps in response to the demands of social discipline always oriented toward the future, toward the achieved self that the educated person has the potential to become. In April 1937, at a moment when the bourgeois ideal of *Bildung* and the concomitant notion of German-Jewish symbiosis lay in ruins, Martin Buber delivered a lecture at the Frankfurt Lehrhaus entitled "Bildung und Weltanschauung." Buber, himself a longtime champion of symbiosis, now voiced reservations about the fixation on the future implicit in *Bildung* and wondered whether the point of departure might not be as important as the point of arrival.[5] Benjamin and Scholem had already been preoccupied with the point of departure two decades earlier. The intellectual line both pursued—Scholem in the actual material he investigated, Benjamin as a kind of model for the organization of temporality—followed the immanent structure of Jewish tradition. Everything originates in the incandescence of revelation, which is then sustained through time in the myriad mirrorings and refractions of exegesis. The whole system is imaginatively focused on the great moment of its origination, however bold and surprising the "spontaneity" of later interpreters. Even the landscape of redemption that is a vital element of the tradition is a projection into the future of the Edenic past reported in revelation. This orientation toward the past differs essentially from the Greek myth of a golden age because its crucial moment is not the myth of Eden but the dynamic event of revelation that makes relentless demands on all subsequent generations, compelling them to construe and absorb its meaning by engaging in a process of continuous interpretation. In this respect, as in several others, our three exemplary German-Jewish modernists, precisely because the idea of Jewish tradition looms over their imaginative worlds, constitute an extreme instance of a common modernist concern—the willed movement of return to traditional roots in a world threatening to dissolve into incoherence that variously characterizes the writing of Joyce, Pound, Eliot, Mann.

One measure of Kafka's imaginative integrity is that he represents this urgent attention to origins without the slightest hint of nostalgia. Let me illustrate by referring to two of his parables, one that deals with the idea of revelation and the

other with the idea of interpretation. "An Imperial Message,"
written in 1917, around the time Kafka began his Hebrew
studies, resembles the classical midrashic parable, or *mashal*, in
exploiting (though only implicitly) a correspondence between
terrestrial monarch and celestial King. The Emperor on his
deathbed whispers to one of his emissaries a message intended, as in a spiritual sense all revelation is intended, "for
you alone." The narrative terms of the parable at first seem
preeminently spatial. At the center is the Emperor in the midst
of his concentric palaces, surrounded by the brilliant solar
insignia of his reign; far out at the periphery, "cowering in the
remotest distance," is the subject for whom the message is
destined. The imperial messenger begins to make his way
from inner to outer chamber, through stairways and passage-
ways and courts, which multiply endlessly and are in turn
surrounded by the almost impenetrable clutter and throngs of
the capital city. Just before the end of the parable, this spatial
representation of the impossibility of delivering the message
becomes temporal as well: the messenger winds his laby-
rinthine way from palace to palace and court to court "and so
on for thousands of years" (*und so weiter durch Jahrtausende*),
bearing a message he will never succeed in delivering, "from a
dead man." The absolute urgency of the message is not in
doubt—it comes, after all, from the Emperor himself, and is
destined for no one but "you," who listen to the story. This,
however, is a parable of revelation enunciated but unconsum-
mated. You surely need the message, languish without it, but
you will never get it. And in contrast to the King-*mashal* of
rabbinic midrash, the fictional vehicle plays a nihilistic—
might it be Nietzschean?—trick on its theological referent,
for the endlessly deferred message comes not from the living
God but, as we realize with a little shock at the end of the
penultimate sentence, from a dead man.[6] "An Imperial Message" thus strikingly illustrates how Kafka is caught up in the
process of tradition, its orientation toward the revelatory,

commanding moment of the past, without permitting himself the least assurance or consolation of tradition.

"The New Advocate," which more explicitly confronts present with past and deals with exegesis rather than with revelation, converts the latter-day disjointedness of tradition into quietly absurd comedy. The advocate of the title is Dr. Bucephalus, the famed charger of Alexander the Great turned into a member of the bar and a student of the law. Much has changed, the narrator notes, since the ancient time when a hero could dream of conquering all the known world. "Nowadays—it cannot be denied—there is no Alexander the Great." One may discover many brandished swords in a landscape of divisiveness and petty treacheries, but no one to lead the way to India. Bucephalus now has no thought of armed clashes and the struggle for empire. "In the quiet lamplight, his flanks unhampered by the thighs of a rider, free and far from the clamor of battle, he reads and turns the pages of our ancient tomes."[7] This concluding image may reflect a half-conscious reminiscence of the fourth book of *Gulliver's Travels*. In any case, it conveys a sense of sad and necessary discrepancies. The grand acts of the past are no longer achievable, and perhaps it is just as well they were renounced, for such renunciation might also mean abandoning the rule of the sword for the less exciting, more civilizing rule of law. If the law is to be applied, it must be carefully studied and understood, which is what Bucephalus undertakes at the end of the parable. But the picture of the quadruped advocate, turning the pages of the ancient tomes with his front hooves, is vaguely risible and does not altogether inspire confidence. What, we wonder, can this old dobbin make of our ancient laws? Even if the imperial message actually reaches us, is there any among us who is confidently capable of construing its meaning?

The bizarre jurist Bucephalus struck Benjamin as an emblem of Kafka's posttraditional world. "The gate to justice is learning," he notes near the end of his essay on Kafka, enunciating a central idea of rabbinic Judaism with specific reference to Bucephalus. But he recognizes that traditional value and practice have here undergone a portentous, probably irreversible transmogrification: "And yet Kafka does not dare attach to this learning the promises which tradition has attached to the study of the Torah. His assistants are sextons who have lost their house of prayer, his students are pupils who have lost their Holy Writ."[8] This last remark, as we shall see presently, triggered an epistolary debate between Benjamin and Scholem on whether the Kafkan protagonists were actually deprived of a Holy Writ, as, for example, "An Imperial Message" suggests, or whether they were rather confronted with a Holy Writ they could not decipher, as one might infer from the concluding image of "The New Advocate." At first blush, the difference between the two positions may seem mere hairsplitting, but it will be worth pondering what might be at stake in the opposition between an absent and an unintelligible revelation.

As a preliminary to that consideration, let us recall the different channels through which the two men worked their way back to the idea of revelation. Scholem's channel was made up of written words, commentaries and supracommentaries going all the way back to the Bible, which is itself a fixed sequence of Hebrew words "deposited in a timeless substratum" sometime in the first millennium B.C.E. Benjamin, as we have abundantly seen, was also fascinated by this very Jewish idea of the truth as writing, but his own imaginative route back to an experience of revelation involved the written word only incidentally. The focus for his thinking about revelation was the concept of aura that repeatedly engaged him during the last eleven years of his life. Aura, as he makes clear in a note to his 1936 essay, "The Work of Art in the Age of Mechanical Reproduction," is strongly associated with the realm of the sacred, representing "the cult value of the work of art."[9] Conceived in spatial terms, aura involves inviolable distance, inapproachability. (The perfect paradigm would be Sinai at the moment of theophany, a promontory suffused with aura: "Take heed to yourselves, that ye go not up into the mountain, or touch the border of it: whosoever toucheth the mount shall be surely put to death", Exodus 19:12.) But Benjamin more characteristically thought of aura in temporal terms; an object imagined is felt to have numinous value, an effect of the sacred, because it is steeped in memory. Thus, in his essay on Baudelaire he defines aura as "the associations which, at home in the *mémoire involontaire*, tend to cluster around the object of perception."[10] The principal arena for the play of aura is thus individual consciousness, not history or collective experience.

There is, however, a set of structural analogies between Benjamin's aura and the revelation on Sinai in thunder and lightning as conceived by Jewish tradition. In both, the potency of the truth is located in the past and has to be captured or "recuperated" from the past (as Benjamin imagines memory in "The Next Village," flashing back like lightning to the revelatory point of origin). In both, truth and value are manifested as an irruption into the realm of the mundane, in no way dictated by human volition—Benjamin associates aura not with memory plain and simple but with involuntary memory, surging from the unconscious. What is remembered, in this fashion, moreover, becomes a kind of inexhaustible semantic wellspring, yielding up endless meanings, much as Scholem would characterize the kabbalistic conception of Torah. "For an experienced event is finite," Benjamin writes in his essay on Proust, "—at any rate, confined to one sphere of experience; a remembered event is infinite, because it is only a key to everything that happened before it and after it."[11]

It follows from this whole emphasis on the epiphanic force of memory that the aesthetic experience in general is before all else the most potent and subtle mnemonic that culture has devised. "Insofar as art aims at the beautiful," Benjamin observes in connection with Baudelaire, "and, on however modest a scale, 'reproduces' it, it conjures it up (as Faust does

Helen) out of the womb of time."[12] The suggestion of a recuperation of some sort of archaic and archetypal past may not sound much like Proust's focus on individual memory, but Benjamin realizes that the Proustian experience involves the revelation of universal laws of human existence, of the relationship of consciousness to temporality as such. What happens on the small scale of revelatory *mémoire involontaire* for the individual also happens on the scale of racial memory, for which the conjuring up of Helen in Goethe's *Faust* stands as emblem. The archaic as a source of authority and aesthetic power has exerted its allure over a good many modernists. If one accepts Benjamin's notion that Kafka's fiction represents a "prehistoric world" of arcane ancestral gestures, then this allure plays its part in Kafka, too. (Benjamin would no doubt have been intrigued by Agnon's 1950 novella "Edo and Enam," in which it is intimated that the main character in effect composes a third part of *Faust* by conjuring up a beautiful enigmatic woman from depths more archaic than Helen's Greece.) Scholem, repeatedly drawn to "abysses," located the allure of the archaic in the experience of Jewish tradition. He did this in a double sense, by uncovering a trail of buried texts that went back through the millennia and, as a kind of archeological philologist, by exposing in Jewish mysticism the workings of repressed ancient myths that antedate monotheism.

Benjamin clearly saw that the memory of what is hidden in the womb of time could manifest itself in a variety of ways, but the way personally accessible to him was aesthetic experience, which he tended to associate with a perception of *déjà vu*—the receiver's end, one might say, of the phenomenon of aura. In his *Moscow Diary*, in the entry for December 23, 1926, after seeing an unusually beautiful Cézanne in a museum, he notes: "It seemed to me that to the extent that one grasps a painting, one does not in any way enter into its space; rather, this space thrusts itself forward, especially in various very specific spots. It opens up to us in corners and angles in which we believe we can localize crucial experiences of the past; there is something inexplicably familiar about these spots."[13] With this personal apprehension of the suggestive power of *déjà vu*, Benjamin saw a collective wisdom, though a wisdom in which he himself could not directly participate, in the orientation of Jewish tradition toward what was revealed in the past. "We know that the Jews were prohibited from investigating the future," he writes at the end of his "Theses on the Philosophy of History." "The Torah and the prayers instruct them in remembrance, however."[14] There were two imaginative steps he found it difficult to take. One was from the Jewish focus on the vista of the past to the Jewish expectation of a future redemption—a paradox he states at the end of his "Theses" without satisfactorily explaining. The other was the step from the private, aesthetic revelation of *déjà vu* to the collective memory of revelation that Jewish tradition took as its matrix. The second of these issues is involved in the debate between him and Scholem over the role of revelation in Kafka's fictional world.

Benjamin and Scholem, as we noted earlier, had had several intense epistolary exchanges on Kafka from the late 1920s onward. During the early summer of 1934, Benjamin sent Scholem a first draft and then a revised version of his essay on Kafka, which appeared later that year in the Zionist newspaper *Jüdische Rundschau*. Given how much the topic mattered to both men, it is hardly surprising that Benjamin should have been passionately interested in Scholem's response to his essay, or that Scholem should have expressed both the keenest enthusiasm and, on one essential point, an objection that bordered on indignation. Scholem had actually raised the issue of revelation in Kafka three years earlier, in the letter of August 1, 1931, in which he spoke of Kafka's "linguistic world" as representing "the prosaic in its most canonical form."[15] There he proposed that Kafka had no real place in German literature (an idea Benjamin seems to have shared, to judge by his Kafka essays) but should be thought of instead against the background of the Book of Job, "in the continuum of Jewish literature." Urging Benjamin to pursue this line in his criticism, he expressed some apprehension—in the event, borne out by what Benjamin would write—that the "critique will become just as esoteric as its subject." (We have seen that Brecht, with his criterion of utility for the masses, was offended by the esotericism.) "The light of revelation," Scholem observed, "never burned as unmercifully as it does here. This is the theological secret of perfect prose." It is characteristic that both Scholem and Benjamin should have expressed themselves on Kafka in terms sufficiently esoteric that each was obliged to question the other about what he really meant, and one can hardly expect that all these difficulties will be laid to rest by a third party. The source and nature of the revelation in Kafka are by no means clear from Scholem's letter, and the only intimation of its content—Scholem is evidently thinking of *The Trial*—is the terse statement that "the Last Judgment is . . . a martial law." But in the exchange with Benjamin over the essay on Kafka, Scholem proposes a still more radical view of the content of revelation. Here is his vehement statement in the letter of July 17, 1934:

Kafka's world is the world of revelation, but of revelation seen of course from that perspective in which it is returned to its own nothingness. I cannot accept your disavowal of this aspect . . . The *nonfulfillability* of what has been revealed is the point where a *correctly* understood theology . . . coincides most perfectly with that which offers the key to Kafka's work. Its problem is not, dear Walter, its *absence* in a preanimistic world, but the fact that it cannot be *fulfilled*. It is about this text that we will have to reach an understanding. Those pupils of whom you speak at the end are not so much those who have lost the Scripture . . . but rather those students who cannot decipher it.[16]

Benjamin understandably wanted clarification on the idea of the nothingness of revelation. At the same time, parrying the esoteric with the esoteric, he appropriated the image himself in his answering letter (July 20, 1934) and spoke inscrutably of Kafka's attempt "to feel his way toward redemption" from within the "inside lining" of nothingness. Whatever he meant by this, he could see no significance in the distinction on which Scholem insisted between absent and unintelligible revelation, as he made clear in a letter written three weeks later (August 11, 1934): "Whether the pupils have lost it [the Scripture] or whether they are unable to decipher it comes down to the same thing, because, without the key that belongs to it, the Scripture is not Scripture, but life. Life as it is lived in the village at the foot of the hill on which the castle is built."[17] Scholem's response of September 20, 1934, comes as close as he will come to explaining the enigma of his idea of revelation and to defending the importance of the distinction between the lost and the indecipherable:

> You ask what I understand by the "nothingness of revelation"? I understand by it a state in which revelation appears to be without meaning, in which it still asserts itself, in which it has *validity* but *no significance*. A state in which the wealth of meaning is lost and what is in the process of appearing (for revelation is such a process) still does not disappear, even though it is reduced to the zero point of its own content, so to speak. This is obviously a borderline case in the religious sense, and whether it can really come to pass is a very dubious point. I certainly cannot share your opinion that it doesn't matter whether the disciples have lost the "Scriptures" or whether they can't decipher them, and I view this as one of the greatest mistakes you could have made. When I speak of the nothingness of revelation, I do so precisely to characterize the difference between these two positions.[18]

There is, let me suggest, a small but critical difference between the formulation here and that in the letter written a month earlier that may reflect a certain ambivalence on Scholem's part and corresponds to the two sides of his paradoxical definition of Kafka as a writer on the borderline between religion and nihilism. The "zero point" of revelation invoked here is religion pushed to the brink of nihilism, and Scholem is doubtful as to "whether it can really come to pass." By contrast, in the letter of July 17, the nothingness and hence the un-fulfillability of revelation in Kafka are construed as an extreme and exemplary instance of what is characterized, with the emphasis of underlining, as "a *correctly* understood theology"—that is, theology in general and not just Kafkan theology. Revelation is not merely an idea of Jewish tradition that Scholem studied as a historian but something he saw with perfect seriousness as an underlying phenomenon of man's creaturely existence. The radical nature of his understanding of revelation is manifested in his sense, buttressed by the Kabbalah, that only the ossified, institutional mechanisms of religion lead us to imagine that revelation has a clearly codifiable content. The notion of nothingness in the letter of July 17, 1934, actually builds on an idea expressed aphoristically in an article that had appeared a year and a half earlier—an aphorism that in fact profoundly impressed Benjamin: "The absolutely concrete can never be fulfilled at all" (see Benjamin's letter of February 28, 1933). Two decades later Scholem would repeat this idea in "Revelation and Tradition" as his definition of revelation and then go on to say: "The Kabbalistic idea of tradition is founded upon the dialectic tension of precisely this paradox: it is precisely the absoluteness that effects the unending reflections in the contingencies of fulfillment."[19] The invocation of nothingness violates conventional assumptions that revelation should be of something definite and definable. Scholem probably had in the back of his mind the kabbalistic cosmogony, in which the Infinite, the *'Eyn Sof*, transposes itself into the created world through the mediation of the *'Ayin*, the divine primordial nothingness. The fact, then, that Kafka's sundry pupils, advocates and students and victims of the law, should be scrutinizing scriptures that defy understanding, is only a modern version of what is the authentic process of receiving revelation at all times—or, to put it in slightly different terms, it is a peering into the shadowy underside of revelation as it is understood in the Kabbalah, however camouflaged that underside may be by the exuberant fecundity of kabbalistic interpretation.

Scholem's essential point in his debate with Benjamin is that the world in which we find ourselves has an ultimate, though also ultimately inscrutable, semantic power: something is always "in the process of appearing" from the ground of being that imposes itself on us with the sheer force of its validity, even if it finally has no safely construable significance. To say that the pupils have simply lost their Holy Writ is to concede what Scholem the religious anarchist was unwilling to concede, that there is no working connection between human consciousness and ultimate being. He repeatedly linked Job with Kafka not only because of the themes of judgment and inscrutable justice but also, I suspect, because of Job's heterodox version of revelation. It is revelation, after all, that "resolves" Job's quandary. When the Lord thunders his poetry from the whirlwind, we are drawn into a dazzling vision of sheer cosmic power, and of the uncanny beauty of power, that shatters human frameworks, including the Bible's own picture of a hierarchical, anthropocentric creation.

When Scholem speaks of the light of revelation burning unmercifully in Kafka's fiction, I think he is actually referring not merely to the fictional representation of the phenomenon of revelation in Kafka but to a registering in "perfect prose" of an *experience of revelation* by Kafka—a revelation that is demanding, elusive, perplexing, pushing toward its intrinsic zero point of overpowering validity coupled with absence of meaning. Such a notion jibes with the idea Kafka proposes in his diary of creating a new Kabbalah, of being assaulted from above as he writes, and it is surely what Scholem had in mind later in his career when he spoke of Kafka as a heretical kabbalist. Scholem, with the model always at hand and close to heart of intense commentary on ancient Hebrew texts exhibiting abysmally polysemous power, could readily conceive Kafka in this way as an exegete of nothingness in a continuous line, if not at the end of the line, of daring Jewish mystics. Benjamin, who in the 1930s was imagining the revelatory force of the past less in the irruption of the absolute into human language and more in the aesthetically triggered efflorescence of aura from the depths of memory, detected no realizations of aura in Kafka's world. What on the contrary caught his eye was Kafka's brilliant dramatization of man's alienation from both self and fellow man, which he pointedly associated with film and photography, procedures of mechanical reproduction he would soon highlight when he wrote about the loss of aura in the modern age. For Benjamin, then, seeing the Kafka protagonist severed from the sacral source of value, including its aesthetic equivalent in aura, it was easy to conceive that the pupils no longer had a Holy Writ, or that if they possessed an indecipherable text that passed for Holy Writ, it amounted to the same thing as not having one at all.

Scholem, Benjamin, and Kafka stood at different points, which did not remain wholly fixed for any of them, in the no-man's-land between religious tradition and modern secular culture; and it is a tricky business to define their location. Scholem devoted his life to the study of religious texts; at least at one juncture, he actually experimented with kabbalistic techniques of trance-inducing meditation; the powerful interpretation of Jewish history that he developed argued implicitly for the abiding validity of the encounter with transcendence that Judaism claimed as its ultimate ground. At the same time, he was an academic student of mysticism, not a mystic himself, as he repeatedly took pains to explain to interviewers; and the intellectual tools with which he sought to grasp Jewish history were the tools of empirical inquiry, linked to a realm of secular value. Benjamin's cast of mind, as Scholem repeatedly insisted, was essentially that of a metaphysician, and he was obviously fascinated by mystical concepts and the lore of Jewish tradition. Although he never entirely discarded these religious interests, after his embrace of Marxism they persisted mainly in a kind of intellectual afterlife as a set of potent concepts, images, and symbols, expressing the deep nostalgia for tradition of a thinker who had placed himself beyond its pale. (One may recall again the plangent closing lines of Scholem's poem on Benjamin's *One-Way Street*: "We are not pious,/We remain in the Profane,/And where God once stood now stands: Melancholy.") Kafka's relation to religious experience is the most acutely paradoxical of the three. Commentators have sometimes reduced his work to autopsychobiography, or to sociopolitical or religious allegory, but he actually undertook a more daring and difficult task in his writing, which was to expose himself to, or take by imaginative force, a realm of the transcendent in which perhaps he could not believe, or, if believed in, which might prove inimical and perverse. Scholem, seeing the "light of revelation" in Kafka's prose, recognized that the tormented novelist had entered into a more immediate confrontation with the theological than either he or Benjamin, and that is ultimately why the two friends perceived him as their "canonical" modern writer. But precisely because of the unflinching immediacy of the confrontation, there is also an aspect of negation of the transcendent, of ruthless satiric exposure of pretenses to the transcendent, in Kafka's writing. That negative aspect is intimated in the second of Scholem's letters to Benjamin on the nothingness of revelation, when he stresses the idea of a zero point and wonders whether such a thing can really happen.

With all this preoccupation with the luminous lore of Jew-

ish tradition, it is not surprising that angels, sometimes explicit
and sometimes disguised, should float through the imaginative
world of the three writers. We may get at least a provisional
sense of where they variously stood in their shared spiritual
no-man's-land by considering a literary sighting of an angel by
each of the three. In 1921 Benjamin acquired Paul Klee's
Angelus Novus, an oil painting colored with aquarelle executed
the previous year. For the rest of his life Benjamin kept the
drawing, according to Scholem's testimony, as a kind of spiritual talisman and focus for meditation. Benjamin willed the
drawing to Scholem, and it hung in the livingroom of the
Scholem home on Abarbanel Street in Jerusalem until 1989,
when it was placed by his widow in the Israel Museum. At one
point in the early 1920s, Benjamin adopted the title of the
drawing as the name for an intellectual journal he proposed to
found. References to Klee's angel crop up repeatedly in the
Benjamin-Scholem correspondence, and on September 19,
1933, Scholem appends to a letter to Benjamin a poem composed of seven rhyming quatrains entitled "Gruss vom Angelus" (Greetings from Angelus).[20] The poem, spoken by the
angel, begins with Klee's artwork ("I hang nobly on the wall")
and then takes us into the angel's musings on his own vocation.
He identifies himself at the outset as *ein Engelsmann,* an angelman, but the human component interests him less than his divine origin, "that world . . . measured, deep, and clear" whose
messenger he is and where, with his backward gaze, he longs
to return. The fifth stanza, which spells out the angel's desire
to go back ("My wing to soar prepared,/I'd happily turn
back"), was taken by Benjamin as the epigraph for the ninth of
his "Theses on the Philosophy of History," which we will
consider momentarily. Scholem's poem stresses the celestial
character of the angel, more *Engel* than *Mann,* and his mission
of annunciation (*verkünden*), and it refuses to turn him into an
allegory of any secular human role or endeavor. In connection

with what we have observed about the idea of revelation,
Scholem's concluding quatrain is especially suggestive:

> *Ich bin ein unsymbolisch Ding*
> *bedeute was ich bin.*
> *Du drehst umsonst den Zauberring*
> *Ich habe keinen Sinn.*
> I am an unsymbolic thing,
> Meaning what I am.
> You turn in vain the magic ring,
> I don't have any sense.

This is a most monotheistic angel, turning against the assumption of mythology (in which angels originate) that reality can
be represented as a network of images and stories conveying
coherent meanings. Scholem's "unsymbolic" angel stubbornly
resists any translation of who he is and what he proclaims into
human systems of meaning. Like revelation in Kafka and the
Kabbalah, he manifests the vocative power of divinity speaking to humankind, but he has no *Sinn*, no sense or significance.

Although angels are traditionally and etymologically, in
both Hebrew and Greek, messengers, as Scholem's poem reminds us, Benjamin's meditation on the *Angelus Novus* in his
ninth Thesis removes the angel from the realm of revelation
and divine messages. This is his complete text:

A Klee painting named "Angelus Novus" shows an angel looking
as though he is about to move away from something he is fixedly
contemplating. His eyes are staring, his mouth is open, his wings
are spread. This is how one pictures the angel of history. His face
is turned toward the past. Where we perceive a chain of events,
he sees one single catastrophe which keeps piling wreckage upon
wreckage and hurls it in front of his feet. The angel would like to
stay, awaken the dead, and make whole what has been smashed.
But a storm is blowing from Paradise; it has got caught in his
wings with such violence that the angel can no longer close them.
This storm irresistibly propels him into the future to which his

back is turned, while the pile of debris before him grows skyward. This storm is what we call progress.[21]

It makes little difference whether one takes the angel the way Benjamin flatly presents him, as a general allegory of un-flinchingly witnessing history—"Where we perceive a chain of events, he sees one single catastrophe"—or whether one sees in him, as Rolf Tiedemann has proposed in a circumspect essay, an image of the historical materialist.[22] What is essential is that the tension between past and future in Benjamin's thinking, which we had occasion to note earlier, is brought to a terrific pitch here, threatening to tear apart what he is trying to imagine about the aim and character of historical process. This picture of history as sky-high wreckage and continuous catastrophe is of course a mirror of the moment: spring 1940, most of Europe in the shadow of the swastika, Stalin and Hitler joined in a covenant of murder. But the awful estrange-ment from a harmonious past, ultimately based on the old Hebrew story of banishment from the Garden, had been a controlling idea of Benjamin's since the 1920s. It is hard not to construe the final sentence, "This storm is what we call prog-ress," as a bitter irony, though the Marxist and the messianist in Benjamin would desperately want to give it a more positive meaning. In any case, the angel, a kind of dumbfounded refugee from the world of religious symbolism, is not located on a vertical axis between the celestial and the terrestrial, as in Scholem's poem, but on a temporal axis between the dream of paradisiacal origins and the unimaginable vista—might it prove simply a nightmare?—of whatever lies at the end of history's long catastrophe. The image here is more drastic, more violent, than the ones invoked in Benjamin's essays on modern literature and culture, but the effect is similar: a focus on the iconography of tradition serves the purpose of defining more sharply the disasters of secular modernity—the erosion of experience, the decay of wisdom, the loss of redemptive vision, and now, in 1940, the universal reign of mass murder. The angel here is not annunciating angelman but witnessing man, allegorically endowed with the terrible power of seeing things utterly devoid of illusion.

Kafka's angel-sighting is recorded in his diary entry for June 25, 1914. Presented as a first-person narrative, it appears to be the draft of a story that he either broke off without finishing or decided not to develop further for publication. The narrator, a tenant in a rented room, has been pacing back and forth in his chamber all day in a mixture of restlessness and boredom. Toward evening, he witnesses an extraordinary event. He perceives a tremor in the plastered white ceiling. Cracks appear, then wave after wave of colors, yellow and golden-yellow, which give the ceiling an eerie transparency. "Things striving to break through seemed to be hovering above it"; then an arm bearing a silver sword is thrust out from above, and the narrator recognizes it as "a vision intended for my liberation." At this point, the crucial second stage of the epiphany occurs. In a violent fit, the narrator leaps up on the table, tears the brass fixture of the electric light from the ceiling, and hurls it to the floor. Immediately afterward, the ceiling breaks open.

> In the dim light, still at a great height, I had judged it badly, an angel in bluish-violet robes girt with gold cords sank slowly down on great white silken-shining wings, the sword in its raised arm thrust out horizontally. "An angel, then!" I thought; "it has been flying towards me all the day and in my disbelief I did not know it. Now it will speak to me." I lowered my eyes. When I raised them again the angel was still there, it is true, hanging rather far under the ceiling (which had closed again), but it was no living angel, only a painted wooden figurehead off the prow of some ship, one of the kind that hangs from the ceiling in sailors' taverns, nothing more.
>
> The hilt of the sword was made in such a way as to hold candles and catch the dripping tallow. I had pulled the electric

light down; I didn't want to remain in the dark, there was still one
candle left, so I got up on a chair, stuck the candle into the hilt of
the sword, lit it, and then sat late into the night under the angel's
faint flame.[23]

Like "An Imperial Message," this is a posttraditional story
quite consciously about revelation, but it differs in actually
recreating the look and feel of the visionary experience together with its frustration. The frustration seems inevitable for
the Kafka protagonist inhabiting a world—as the early rabbis
said of their own reality—that has irrevocably lost the gift of
prophecy. Generically, one might describe this text as a narrative of angelic epiphany that turns into a shaggy-dog story.
The initial revelation of the angel is accompanied by all the
traditional paraphernalia: seismic vibrations, iridescent colors,
an access of frenzy in the beholder, an outthrust silver sword,
the angel itself in splendid robes with shining wings. Kafka's
angel, though expected to bring a message of liberation, bears
a sword (like the Statue of Liberty in the opening paragraph of
Amerika), for Kafka was scarcely capable of imagining an image
of redemption or gratification that did not also harbor a
potential threat. In this particular instance, the sword is also
determined by an iconographic tradition that goes back to the
angel with the sword set at the gates of Eden when Adam and
Eve were banished. This angel, like Benjamin's, might perhaps
be a refugee from paradise, but without the capacity to look
back: it stands in precisely the sad relation to the realm of
divine origins as that in which a wooden figurehead nailed to
the ceiling of a tavern stands to the sea.
    The dynamics of manifestation to which Kafka devotes
loving attention in the first part of the story are a vivid
illustration of Scholem's minimal definition of revelation as
something "in the process of appearing." What finally appears,
of course, is nothing that can speak to the narrator, as he
desperately desires, but a block of carved wood, a mere human

artifact, and a rather crude one at that. The sharpness of the disappointment is underscored by the downward translation from realm to realm: not only is the celestial figure seen to be purely terrestrial, but the figurehead itself looks like one of those that have been removed from the great open kingdom of the sea to the mundane, and perhaps somewhat sordid, sphere of a sailors' tavern. The narrative that began in high theological dignity becomes a painful farce. In the terms of the Kafka parable we looked at earlier, the prospective Abraham, on the brink of an angelic visitation, turns into not Don Quixote but Sancho Panza, perfectly aware that the giant is only a creaking windmill, that Dulcinea is a greasy peasant girl with garlic on her breath. The angel, with its fleeting promise of revelation, is associated with cultural memory but is discovered to be only a relic from the past, an accoutrement of a vanished era of seafaring put to decorative use in the age of Edison.

But it is characteristic of Kafka, as a posttraditionalist who nevertheless somehow wrote "in the light of revelation," that the story does not stop here. The narrator, having torn out the modern, technological source of illumination in the room, does not want to remain enveloped in darkness. (However minimal the narrative report, this image of seeking light in darkness has strong archetypal reverberations and recalls a host of biblical verses, from Psalms and elsewhere: "The Lord will light up my darkness," "A lamp of God is man's soul," "The people walking in darkness saw a great light," and so forth.) If the angel, exposed as a lifeless thing, cannot actively provide spiritual illumination, it can be made an implement for shedding light. Thus the narrator takes his single candle, fixes it in the hilt of the angel's sword, and sits—doing what, we cannot know—"late into the night under the angel's faint flame." The story ends, if this is in fact the intended ending, with no shred of illusion about the angel's true character. Nevertheless, a hint of paradoxical reversal, *Umkehr*, hovers over the conclusion. There has been, after all, some kind of miraculous manifestation, even if it turned into a wooden disappointment. The faint flame that provides the narrator flickering comfort through the dark of the night is identified not as the candle's but as the angel's. Technically, this is a simple metonymic substitution of a sort common in ordinary speech. But its very position as the final phrase and the concluding image of the story lends it a certain weight of implication. The angel, mere popular artifact that it has proved to be, provides light, though faint, for the soul in darkness.

The wry gesture is quintessentially Kafkan, and it is hard to imagine another modern writer capable of reproducing it convincingly. (Beckett might have imagined the wooden angel, but in his world the wick would not have held the flame.) As an emblem, however, of that form of modern Jewish writing which is, in Kafka's own memorable phrase, "an assault on the frontiers," the man sitting late into the night by the angel's dim light is an apt figure not only for Kafka's enterprise but also for Benjamin's and Scholem's. All three, turning from the complacencies of German bourgeois assimilationism, were fascinated by the world of Jewish origins with its unfathomable theological depths. All three feared there could be no real return to origins, that where God once stood there was now only Melancholy. Nevertheless, they variously felt there was no adequate modern substitute for the richly layered spiritual vocabulary that the bearers of tradition had developed in their quest for the truth—surely not in technology, not in science, not in aestheticism, not in psychoanalysis, not in Marxism, even for Benjamin. They were left with a lifelong meditation on the ideas and acts and images of tradition, on the actual text of the Bible, the idea of Torah, the process of commentary, the age-old stories of the Garden, the patriarch and the sacrificial knife, the mountain of revelation, the promise of the Messiah. Thus the figure of an angel could become the vehicle for imagining the paradoxical nothingness of revelation; the tempestuous banishment of humankind from paradise into history; the illusoriness of hoped-for vision, and its pale persistence. Kafka's silent angel speaks neither Hebrew nor German, but it is made, through a willed act of human intervention, to hold a candle for the man to whom it has appeared. As in *The Castle* and in many of the parables, as in the great sweep of Scholem's historiography, as in Benjamin's gnomic reflections on Kafka himself and on other writers, something that may endure still glimmers forth from the realm of transcendence that tradition so urgently addressed.

NOTES

INDEX

NOTES

1. CORRESPONDING ABOUT KAFKA

1. Walter Benjamin, *Briefe*, ed. G. Scholem and T. Adorno (Frankfurt, 1966).
2. The German original is *Walter Benjamin/Gershom Scholem Briefwechsel 1933–1940* (Frankfurt, 1980). The English version, from which all quotations are taken, is *The Correspondence of Walter Benjamin and Gershom Scholem 1932–1940*, trans. Gary Smith and Andre Lefevere (New York, 1989) (hereafter cited as *Benjamin-Scholem Correspondence*).
3. *Benjamin-Scholem Correspondence*, p. 255.
4. Walter Benjamin, *Illuminations*, trans. Harry Zohn (New York, 1968), p. 177.
5. For a patient, pious reconstruction of Benjamin's eccentrically Marxist project, see Susan Buck-Morss, *The Dialects of Seeing: Walter Benjamin and the Arcades Project* (Cambridge, Mass., 1989).
6. Harold Bloom, *Ruin the Sacred the Truths* (Cambridge, Mass., 1989), p. 168.
7. *Jüdische Rundschau*, April 4, 1928, p. 202.
8. The story is found in S. Y. Agnon, *The Complete Stories* (Hebrew), vol. 2 (Tel Aviv, 1953), pp. 361–364. My translations.
9. Gershom Scholem, *Walter Benjamin: The Story of a Friendship*, trans. Harry Zohn (Philadelphia, 1981), pp. 169–174.
10. *Benjamin-Scholem Correspondence*, p. 81.

2. ON NOT KNOWING HEBREW

1. Yehuda Amichai, "Shir Zemani," in *Gam ha'egrof hayah pa'am yad petuhah ve'etsba'ot* (Tel Aviv, 1989), p. 139. My translation.
2. The text of the letter has been published in Betty Scholem and Gershom Scholem, *Mutter und Sohn in Briefwechsel, 1917–1946* (Munich, 1989), p. 13.

3. Franz Kafka, *Letters to Friends, Family, and Editors*, trans. Richard Winston and Clara Winston (New York, 1977), pp. 288–289.

4. Gershom Scholem, ʿOd Davar (Tel Aviv, 1989), p. 53.

5. Ibid., pp. 58–59.

6. The Hebrew original was published in *Kneset*, 2 (1937), 347–392. The English translation is in Gershom Scholem, *The Messianic Idea in Judaism* (New York, 1971), pp. 78–141.

7. For a portrait of Thieberger, see Johannes Urzidil, *There Goes Kafka*, trans. H. A. Basilius (Detroit, 1968), pp. 97–118.

8. Kafka, *Letters to Friends*, p. 390.

9. Ibid., p. 395.

10. Gershom Scholem, *From Berlin to Jerusalem*, trans. Harry Zohn (New York, 1980), p. 79.

11. Franz Kafka, *Letters to Felice*, trans. James Stern and Elizabeth Duckworth (New York, 1973), p. 505.

12. Gershom Scholem, *Walter Benjamin: The Story of a Friendship*, trans. Harry Zohn (Philadelphia, 1981), pp. 137, 138.

13. Leo Lowenthal makes a similar observation on Benjamin's decision to stay in Paris in "The Integrity of the Intellectual: In Memory of Walter Benjamin," in *Benjamin: Philosophy, Aesthetics, History*, ed. Gary Smith (Chicago, 1989), p. 252.

14. Walter Benjamin, *Reflections*, trans. Edmund Jephcott (New York, 1986), pp. 322, 331.

15. Walter Benjamin, *Briefe*, ed. G. Scholem and T. Adorno (Frankfurt, 1966), 2:830–831.

16. Franz Kafka, *The Complete Stories*, ed. N. N. Glatzer (New York, 1971), p. 433.

17. Ibid., p. 434.

18. Ibid., pp. 400–401.

19. Franz Kafka, *The Diaries, 1910–1923*, ed. Max Brod, trans. Joseph Kresh and Martin Greenberg (New York, 1948–49), p. 29.

20. Speech to the Bavarian Academy of the Arts, reproduced in ʿOd Davar, pp. 59–60.

3. THE POWER OF THE TEXT

1. Walter Benjamin, *Reflections*, trans. Edmund Jephcott (New York, 1986), p. 66.

2. Gershom Scholem, ʿ*Od Davar* (Tel Aviv, 1989), p. 304.

3. I am grateful to Professor Michael A. Meyer of the Hebrew Union College, Cincinnati, for this apt suggestion about what may have been behind Scholem's choice of canonical texts.

4. Franz Kafka, *The Diaries, 1910–1923*, ed. Max Brod, trans. Joseph Kresh and Martin Greenberg (New York, 1948–49), p. 215.

5. Franz Kafka, *Parables and Paradoxes*, ed. N. N. Glatzer (New York, 1961), pp. 43–45.

6. Stanley Corngold, *Franz Kafka: The Necessity of Form* (Ithaca, 1988), p. 233.

7. Franz Kafka, *The Castle*, trans. Willa Muir and Edwin Muir (New York, 1969), pp. 7–8.

8. Marthe Robert, *The Old and the New: From Don Quixote to Kafka*, trans. Carol Cosman (Berkeley, 1976).

9. Walter Benjamin, *Illuminations*, trans. Harry Zohn (New York, 1968), p. 147.

10. Benjamin, *Reflections*, p. 68.

11. Ibid., p. 269.

12. Gershom Scholem, *Walter Benjamin: The Story of a Friendship*, trans. Harry Zohn (Philadelphia, 1981), pp. 124–125.

13. Walter Benjamin, *The Origin of German Tragic Drama*, trans. John Osborne (London, 1977), p. 175.

14. Ibid., p. 53.

15. Benjamin, *Illuminations*, p. 257.

16. Ibid., pp. 257, 258–259.

17. Quoted in David Biale, *Gershom Scholem: Kabbalah and Counter-History* (Cambridge, 1979), p. 76. The translation is Biale's; the German text of the letter is reproduced in ibid., pp. 215–216.

18. Gershom Scholem, *The Messianic Idea in Judaism* (New York, 1971), p. 289.

19. Ibid., p. 290.

20. Ibid., pp. 295, 296.

21. Ibid., p. 287.

22. Ibid., p. 303.

23. Richard Wolin aptly observes in *Walter Benjamin: An Aesthetic Redemption* (New York, 1982) that in Benjamin there is no neat division between a metaphysical phase and a Marxist phase because concerns and ideas of the earlier period continue to manifest themselves in the later years.

24. Gershom Scholem, "Zehn unhistorische Sätze über Kabbala," in *Judaica*, vol. 3 (Frankfurt, 1973), p. 271.
25. Kafka, *Parables and Paradoxes*, p. 83.

4. REVELATION AND MEMORY

1. Walter Benjamin, *Reflections*, trans. Edmund Jephcott (New York, 1986), p. 208.
2. Franz Kafka, *The Complete Stories*, ed. N. N. Glatzer (New York, 1971), p. 404.
3. Benjamin, *Reflections*, p. 209.
4. Ibid., pp. 209–210.
5. Cited in George Mosse, *German Jews beyond Judaism* (Bloomington, 1985), p. 36.
6. Kafka, *The Complete Stories*, pp. 4–5.
7. Ibid., p. 415.
8. Walter Benjamin, *Illuminations*, trans. Harry Zohn (New York, 1968), p. 139.
9. Ibid., p. 245.
10. Ibid., p. 188.
11. Ibid., p. 204.
12. Ibid., p. 189.
13. Walter Benjamin, *Moscow Diary*, trans. Richard Sieburth (Cambridge, Mass., 1986), p. 42.
14. Benjamin, *Illuminations*, p. 266.
15. The letter is reproduced by Scholem in *Walter Benjamin: The Story of a Friendship*, trans. Harry Zohn (Philadelphia, 1981), pp. 169–174.
16. *Benjamin-Scholem Correspondence*, pp. 126–127; the emphases are Scholem's.
17. Ibid., p. 135.
18. Ibid., p. 142; the emphases are Scholem's.
19. Gershom Scholem, *The Messianic Idea in Judaism*, (New York, 1971), p. 296.
20. The German text of the poem, preceded by a somewhat ungainly English translation, appears in *Benjamin-Scholem Correspondence*, pp. 79–81. The lines quoted in the text are my own translation.
21. Benjamin, *Illuminations*, pp. 259–260.
22. Rolf Tiedemann, "Historical Materialism or Messianism? An Inter-

pretation of the Theses 'On the Concept of History," in *Benjamin: Philosophy, Aesthetics, History,* ed. Gary Smith (Chicago, 1989), pp. 175–209.

23. Franz Kafka, *The Diaries, 1910–1923,* ed. Max Brod, trans Joseph Kresh and Martin Greenberg (New York, 1948–49), pp. 291–292.

INDEX

Adorno, Gretel, 47, 50, 51

Adorno, Theodor, 5, 47

Agnon, S. Y., 13–15; "Edo and Enam," 105; "The Great Synagogue," 15–17

Amichai, Yehuda, 27–28

Angelus Novus (Klee), 67, 98, 113–116

Assimilation, 4, 22, 27, 28, 30, 32, 99–100, 119

Baudelaire, Charles, 9–10, 80, 82, 104

Bauer, Felice, 41, 42

Beckett, Samuel, 61, 119

Benjamin, Dora, 4, 35

Benjamin, Emil, 30, 49

Benjamin, Walter: on apprehending the past, 81–84, 115; Arcades project, 9–10, 45; aura, 103–106, 111; correspondence, 4–6, 8, 11, 106, 108, 109, 113; dreams, 47–52, 59; early friendship with Scholem, 3–4, 6; on exegesis, 68–69, 79–84, 100; on Hebrew, 45–46, 81, 99; on Kafka, 12, 18–21, 22, 79, 95–99, 102–103, 106–111; on language, 45–46, 50, 80–81; "On Language as Such and the Language of Man," 46, 53; Marxism, 3, 8, 10, 43–44, 83, 99, 115, 119; *Moscow Diary*, 105–106; *One-Way Street*, 19, 80, 112; *The Origin of German Tragic Drama*, 34, 82; on origins, 98, 100; on revelation, 103–111; suicide, 5, 6, 10, 48–49; student of Hebrew, 40–45; "The Task of the Translator," 46; on tex-

tuality, 62, 67–68; "Theses on the Philosophy of History," 83–84, 87, 99, 113, 114–116; on tradition, 82, 84, 119–120; "The Work of Art in the Age of Its Mechanical Reproduction," 103

Bergmann, Hugo, 39, 41–42

Biale, David, 83

Bible, 54–55, 69, 72–76, 106–107, 108, 110, 117, 118

Bloom, Harold, 12, 89

Borges, J. L., 97

Bourgeoisie, 31, 37, 42, 43, 99–100

Brecht, Bertolt, 4, 34, 95–97

Brenner, Y. H., 40

Broch, Hermann, 61

Brod, Max, 32, 39, 42

Buber, Martin, 90, 100

Buck-Morss, Susan, 123n5

Canonicity, 19, 69–70, 71–72, 108–109

Commentary. *See* Exegesis

Corngold, Stanley, 76

Don Quixote, 73–75, 79, 118

Dyamant, Dora, 39

Eliot, T. S., 100

Exegesis, 17, 63, 68–92, 100

Faust (Goethe), 105

Flaubert, Gustave, 19, 31, 34

Fragmentariness, 10–11, 82, 83

Fromm, Erich, 90

German, 28–30, 32–35, 51, 53, 59, 60–61
Graetz, Heinrich, 35, 39
Gulliver's Travels (Swift), 102

Hebrew, 8, 27–63, 88–89
History. *See* Benjamin: on apprehending the past; Scholem: on apprehending the past
Hofmannsthal, Hugo von, 44

Inscription, 27–28, 48–52, 56–60, 62–63, 67–68, 82, 99
Interpretation. *See* Exegesis

Joyce, James, 61, 62, 100

Kabbalah, 12, 18, 35, 45, 56, 63, 71, 87, 109, 110; *Zohar*, 69
Kafka, Franz: and Agnon, 13–14, 17, 18–19; *Amerika*, 53, 76, 117; "The Animal in the Synagogue," 53; on the Bible, 72–76; *The Castle*, 19, 53, 76–79; "The City Coat of Arms," 54–56; comic elements in, 21–23, 74–75, 76, 79, 102; correspondence, 32–33, 68; *Diaries*, 39, 60, 70–72, 116–119; "A Dream," 56–60; on exegesis, 71–79, 87, 91–92, 102, 103; "An Imperial Message," 101–102; "In the Penal Colony," 68; "Josephine the Singer," 54; "The Judgment," 59, 70; on language, 54–55; *Letter to His Father*, 29, 32; as modernist, 12, 58, 69; "The New Advocate," 102–103; "The Next Village," 95–99; on origins, 100–102, 105; "The Pit of Babel," 74, 75; "Prometheus," 91–92; on revelation, 91, 101–102, 117–119; student of Hebrew, 32, 38–42; on textuality,

71, 79; *The Trial*, 53, 56, 60, 76, 107; view of Hebrew, 42; on writing, 33
Kafka, Hermann, 29, 32, 59
Klee, Paul. *See Angelus Novus*
Kleist, Wilhelm von, 34
Klopstock, Robert, 40
Kraus, Karl, 32, 34, 80, 81

Langer, Georg, 39
Language, 27–63
Lowenthal, Leo, 90, 124n13

Magnes, Judah, 44, 81
Mann, Thomas, 100
Memory, 97–98, 104–106, 118
Meyer, Michael A., 125n3
Midrash, 72, 75, 101
Modernism, 31–32, 34, 58, 61–62, 84, 100, 105
Modernity, 21–22, 68, 84, 115–116
Mosse, George, 99

Past, apprehension of. *See under* Benjamin; Scholem
Pines, M. I., 39
Pound, Ezra, 100
Proust, Marcel, 61, 80, 82, 97, 104, 105

Reichmann, Frieda, 90
Revelation, 17, 18, 72, 91, 101–120
Robert, Marthe, 78
Rosenzweig, Franz, 6, 35, 36, 90

Sartre, J.-P., *The Family Idiot*, 31
Schocken, Salman, 12, 85
Scholem, Arthur, 29–30, 31
Scholem, Escha, 39
Scholem, Gershom: on apprehending the past, 84–89; boyhood, 30; correspondence, 6, 7–8, 107, 108, 113; early friendship with Benjamin, 3–4; on exegesis, 69–70, 84–89, 100;

From Berlin to Jerusalem, 7, 30; "Gruss vom Angelus," 113–114; on Hebrew, 35–38, 88–89; on Kafka, 18–19, 22, 69, 106–111, 112; *Major Trends in Jewish Mysticism*, 9, 29; as modernist, 84; on origins, 100, 105; *Origins of the Kabbalah*, 29, 88; "Redemption through Sin," 37–38; on revelation, 85, 87–88, 91–92, 100, 106–111; "Revelation and Tradition as Religious Categories in Judaism," 85–89, 109; *Sabbatai Sevi*, 29, 38; student of Hebrew, 35; "Ten Unhistorical Theses on the Kabbalah," 12, 90–91; on textuality, 85–89; on tradition, 84–89, 119–120; *Walter Benjamin, The Story of a Friendship*, 4, 18

Scholem, Siegfried, 30

Script. *See* Inscription

Surrealism, 9–10, 82

Textuality, 62, 67–68, 71–72, 79, 80–82, 85–89

Thieberger, Friedrich, 39

Tiedemann, Rolphe, 115

Wolin, Richard, 125n23

Zionism, 4, 7, 8, 30, 31, 35, 37, 39, 41, 71–72, 90

Library of Congress Cataloging-in-Publication Data

Alter, Robert.
Necessary angels : tradition and modernity in Kafka, Benjamin,
and Scholem / Robert Alter.
p.   cm.
Includes bibliographical references and index.
ISBN 0-674-60663-9
1. German literature—20th century—History and criticism.
2. German literature—Jewish authors—History and criticism.
3. Kafka, Franz, 1883–1924—Criticism and interpretation.
4. Benjamin, Walter, 1892–1940—Criticism and interpretation.
5. Scholem, Gershom Gerhard, 1897–   —Criticism and interpretation.
6. Jews—Germany—Intellectual life.
7. Jews—Germany—Cultural assimilation.   I. Title.
PT405.A473   1991
830.9'8924'0904—dc20
90-46478
CIP